Praise for *The Happiness Policy Handbook*

Whether you're new to happiness science and the happiness movement or have been on board for a while like me, and whether you're an elected official, policymaker or ordinary citizen, you're bound to learn a great deal and be inspired by this short but clear and helpful book. Bhutan's revolutionary concept of Gross National Happiness is well-explained here, with its multiple "domains" of wellbeing and its highly useful policy tools that can offer guidelines for leaders at every level of government. Written by three leaders in policy, community development, and the happiness movement, this book offers powerful reasons for getting involved with happiness science and making happiness—instead of GDP growth—the goal of government, as Thomas Jefferson once declared it should be. Read it, and then...put it into practice!

— John de Graaf, co-author, *Affluenza: The All-Consuming Epidemic*,
and co-founder, The Happiness Alliance

I am a strong advocate for practical and value-added solutions that organizations can use to make a difference. I see the Happiness Movement at the individual and societal levels as a companion to the Sustainability Movement in the business community. Businesses need to help governments create the requisite conditions for societal happiness and wellbeing. This book shows governments how and why to apply happiness criteria to its processes to create a more socially just, economically inclusive, and environmentally restorative society. If governments required businesses to report on their contributions to those ends, we would dramatically accelerate our journey toward a happy, resilient and truly sustainable society. Hoorah to Musikanski, Phillips, and Crowder, and for showing us the way!

— Bob Willard, author, *The New Sustainability Advantage*
and *Sustainability ROI Workbook*

The pursuit of happiness was enshrined in America's Declaration of Independence and, more recently, in Bhutan's pursuit of Gross National Happiness. It may be tempting to dismiss all of this as wishful thinking, but if we want the world to embrace sustainability, happiness and sustainability have to become two sides of the same coin. I recommend this book as a guide to how this might be done.

— John Elkington, author, *The Breakthrough Challenge*,
Co-Founder and Chief Pollinator at Volans,
Co-Founder of SustainAbility, and
long-time champion of the Triple Bottom Line

The future of governance is in happiness and wellbeing more than in economics and finance. This book will be handy for development experts, project managers, legislators, policymakers, and community and corporate leaders. It provides templates that can be adapted locally.

— Dasho Karma Ura, President,
The Centre for Bhutan Studies
and GNH Research

The Happiness Policy Handbook is a great overview of wellbeing and happiness activity taking place globally—so far—linking to Sustainable Development Goals and positive psychology and how to bring the learning into our collective decision making.

— Nancy Hey, Director, What Works Centre for Wellbeing

The Dubai government has always kept the happiness and welfare of its residents at the core of any strategies or policies launched. I am proud to share our story as part of this book which provides clear and concise step-by-step actions to help governments across the globe implement citizen-centric policies, ensuring greater happiness of their people.

—Dr. Aisha Bin Bishr, Director General of Smart Dubai

The Happiness Policy Handbook

The
Happiness
Policy
HANDBOOK

HOW TO MAKE
HAPPINESS AND WELL-BEING
THE PURPOSE OF YOUR GOVERNMENT

Laura Musikanski ✦ Rhonda Phillips ✦ Jean Crowder

new society
PUBLISHERS

Cover design by Diane McIntosh.
Cover Image © iStock.

Printed in Canada. First printing September 2019.

Inquiries regarding requests to reprint all or part of *The Happiness Policy Handbook*
should be addressed to New Society Publishers at the address below. To order
directly from the publishers, please call toll-free (North America) 1-800-567-6772,
or order online at www.newsociety.com

Any other inquiries can be directed by mail to:

New Society Publishers
P.O. Box 189, Gabriola Island, BC V0R 1X0, Canada

(250) 247-9737

LIBRARY AND ARCHIVES CANADA CATALOGUING IN PUBLICATION

Title: The happiness policy handbook : how to make happiness and well-being
the purpose of your government / Laura Musikanski, Rhonda Phillips, Jean Crowder.

Names: Musikanski, Laura, 1964– author. | Phillips, Rhonda, author. |
Crowder, Jean, 1952– author.

Description: Includes bibliographical references and index.

Identifiers: Canadiana (print) 20190127600 | Canadiana (ebook) 20190127619 |
ISBN 9780865719248 (softcover) | ISBN 9781550927177 (PDF) |
ISBN 9781771423137 (EPUB)

Subjects: LCSH: Happiness—Government policy—Handbooks, manuals, etc. |
LCSH: Happiness—Political aspects—Handbooks, manuals, etc. | LCSH: Well-
being—Government policy—Handbooks, manuals, etc. | LCSH: Well-being—Political
aspects—Handbooks, manuals, etc. | LCGFT: Handbooks and manuals.

Classification: LCC HN25 .M87 2019 | DDC 306—dc23

Funded by the   Financé par le
Government   gouvernement
of Canada   du Canada

New Society Publishers' mission is to publish books that contribute in fundamental
ways
to building an ecologically sustainable and just society, and to do so with the least
possible
impact on the environment, in a manner that models this vision.

DEDICATION

We wrote this book out of a deep belief
in the power of change through positive action,
and so we dedicate this book to you, our readers,
because we believe that collectively we can realize
the happiness movement. Together and individually,
we have demonstrated that there is tremendous capacity
for shaping our world. We believe that you,
with others, can and will shape our world
where all beings have equal opportunity
to pursue happiness.

Contents

Acknowledgments

Our colleagues the world over have inspired us and enabled us to complete this book. It is never enough to say thank you and we hope that our colleagues, family and friends know how very much they mean to us. All of you have certainly increased our happiness!

Authors' Welcome

Welcome to *The Happiness Policy Handbook*. This book provides policymakers, community organizers, and others concerned with present conditions and the future, the means to join the happiness movement. Together we can make a vital difference so that all people have equal opportunities to pursue happiness.

Our hope is that once you have read this book, you will have formed a thorough plan for making happiness the purpose of your government. Over two centuries ago, Thomas Jefferson said "the purpose of government is to enable the people of a nation to live in safety and happiness," but until now there has not always been a clear path for realizing this vision. *The Happiness Policy Handbook* is the first book to present easy-to-use action plans for integrating happiness and well-being into governmental processes and institutions. The book includes explanations, graphics, and forms for you to adapt and implement. It is divided into two sections. In the first section, you will learn about the landscape of the happiness movement, including its history, roots, and trajectory. The second section provides accessible action plans, with tools and resources that can be used sequentially or individually as needed. The action plans in the second section can be adapted to fit the circumstances of an area and situation by any level of policymaker, from a president to a governor, mayor, council member, or departmental manager.

To the authors' knowledge, no other book quite like this one has been written. Our hope is that, together, we make history and create a world where all people have equal opportunities to their inalienable right to the pursuit of happiness.

Introduction

The intent of *The Happiness Policy Handbook* is to provide a clear, cohesive, and comprehensive guide for current and future policymakers, and community organizers who believe that the primary purpose of government is to secure people's inalienable right to the pursuit of happiness. It gives simple explanations rooted in scientific evidence and on-the-ground applied experience.

The Happiness Policy Handbook is inspired by a passionate belief that the happiness, well-being, and sustainability of all life on our beautiful planet is possible today and in our future. As a species, humans have a tremendous capacity for shaping the surface of our Earth, changing our climate, building environments, and forming societies. Indeed, we are now in an age that some call the Anthropocene epoch[1]—the era of significant human impact on the Earth's ecosystems. Our capacity to destroy our environment and each other can and should be equally met by our capacity to live harmoniously with each other in an ecologically sustainable manner. With an understanding of the human potential for goodness, compassion, and caring, *The Happiness Policy Handbook* is written to enable and empower policymakers to set the conditions for happiness and well-being for all and for the ecological sustainability of our planet.

A basic tenet of the happiness movement is that the purpose of government is to secure conditions providing people equal opportunity to pursue happiness and to live a good life. Securing the conditions that afford people the opportunity to pursue happiness is very different from dictating behaviors or forcing people to be happy. What makes a person happy and how they pursue their happiness is unique to each person.

The happiness movement represents a new way of governing and living. It is founded on the knowledge that happiness and well-being are grounded in many factors that extend into our natural, built, economic, social, cultural, and personal environments. It was inspired in reaction to the use of gross domestic product (GDP), the sum of all goods and services produced in a year in an economy, as the primary measure guiding policy in many of the world's countries, in addition to a belief that humans have the capacity to govern for the happiness of our species, well-being of society, and environmental health of our planet. When a government sets the goal of increasing the happiness of its people, part of the process is to assess and understand people's current state of happiness. Through this assessment, governments can identify the policies and programs that will best provide opportunities for all people to pursue their happiness.

On a local and global scale, there is renewed interest in policies that secure happiness, such as ensuring equal and adequate opportunities for employment, access to mental and physical health care, access to education, and adequate housing. People are starting to understand that securing today's and future generations' access to a clean and healthy natural environment, fair economies, resilient communities, and personal flourishing, as well as many other factors that contribute to happiness and well-being is *as much as or more important than* economic growth and consumption.

From leaders of nations to city mayors, it is becoming clear to policymakers that protracted placement of economic growth as the predominant goal of nations and states has resulted in widening gaps between human wealth versus human health, commercial rights versus human rights, and distrust versus engagement in the political process. Policymakers everywhere are starting to understand that prioritizing economic policy at the expense of other needs has led to decreases in quality of life for all people, rich or poor. Other needs that need to hold priority encompass such areas as access to education, decent housing, decent paying jobs for all, mental and physical health, rewarding employment, safety in one's neighborhood, social cohesion, social justice, strong families, time balance, trust in one's government, and not least of all, a sustainable environment.

Policymakers worldwide are looking for new ways to secure the happiness of people, well-being of communities, and sustainability of natural systems. Wider measurements of well-being are revealing important information that points the way for policymakers and allows them to understand how to prioritize happiness, well-being, and sustainability. Based on happiness data, policymakers have a new understanding of why economic growth is not the only suitable goal by itself, but just one among many means of influencing people's happiness.

The ultimate outcomes of the happiness movement will be assessed through the many aspects of life that are important to well-being and happiness. Grounded in science and common sense, these aspects are outlined as:

+ *Compassionate communities* with happiness education and loving families in which children grow up with a sense of purpose, meaning, worthiness, positivity, optimism, and agency and become resilient adults who flourish in life;
+ *Ethical, accountable, and accessible government* that puts safeguarding people's inalienable right to life, liberty, and the pursuit of happiness before any other goal, and measures these goals with happiness instruments;
+ *Fair economies* in which all people have equitable opportunities for meaningful work and to address their needs through policies and socially just public-private sector partnerships;
+ *Just societies* in which all people fully experience basic human rights, are treated with respect and dignity, provided strong

safety nets, and have equal access to the resources needed to meet their needs to survive and thrive; and

+ *Thriving natural environments* in which the air, soil, and water is clean and abundant; people have access to nature; biodiversity is preserved and restored where needed; and natural resources are managed safely and sustainably for today and future generations.

The Origins of the Happiness Policy Handbook

We are inspired by the policymakers and community organizers who have been using the Happiness Alliance's Happiness Index since 2011. Over and over, they have requested guidance on how to integrate happiness measurements, data, and policies into government. In reply, many resources and tools have been developed, and many lessons learned. This handbook draws from these lessons learned over the years and organizes the tools and resources that have proven useful to policymakers into a set of easy-to-use implementable actions.

Ample research in quality of life, well-being, happiness, and sustainable development studies demonstrates that happiness policies, programs, and projects result in greater well-being and happiness for people. The range of policies that increase happiness and well-being is vast. It includes economic policies that ensure adequate incomes and low Gini coefficients (these are numerical measures of income inequality at national or sub-national levels); workplace policies that ensure work-life balance and rewarding jobs; housing and transportation policies that ensure adequate housing, green infrastructure, and low commute times; governance policies that foster trust and participation in governmental processes; health policies that promote access to mental and physical health care; social policies that strengthen safety nets, relationships, and community belonging; and many other policies impacting other areas of life.

A growing number of publications and events are educating and inspiring policymakers by providing evidence and ideas for happiness policies, programs, and projects. Important publications in the happiness movement include the *Global Happiness Policy Report*[2] and *World Happiness Reports*[3] which are raising awareness and showcasing happiness research findings. Books such as *Well-Being for Public Policy* (Oxford University Press, 2009) and *The Origins of Happiness* (Princeton University Press, 2018) are providing guidance for policymakers based on valuable findings. These publications should be read and considered by the policymaker when using this book. Some momentous events in the happiness movement are the United Nations High-Level Meeting Well-being and Happiness: Defining a New Economic Paradigm,[4] the annual gatherings held in the United Arab Emirates (UAE) in Dubai called the Global Dialogue for Happiness, the London School of Economics' "Subjective well-being over the life course" event,[5] and the Organization of Economic Co-operation and Development (OECD) World Forums on Statistics, Knowledge, and Policy. Attending future events held by the OECD, the UAE, and others should be considered opportunities for learning and connecting with people in the happiness and well-being movements.

However, to date, there is no one publication that lays out what is needed so that policymakers can take action based on the findings presented in these publications and the learning and information provided at these events. *The Happiness Policy Handbook* seeks to fill these gaps. We base our book's information on the principle that once happiness and well-being are understood and integrated into the processes and institutions of government, then naturally policies will be promulgated, programs adapted or formed, and projects undertaken that realize the goals of happiness and well-being.

A Roadmap to the Handbook

The Happiness Policy Handbook has two major sections. The first provides an overview, or landscape, of the happiness movement and is written for the reader who is seeking to quickly gain a strong grasp of the movement. Section One starts by giving the reader an understanding both of what the happiness movement is and what happiness policy is. It explains the connections between the happiness movement and allied movements—the sustainability movement and the positive psychology movement. While most of us are aware of the rise of the sustainability movement (often referred to in academia as seeking balance between "the three E's—equity, economy, and environment," and in business as measuring and managing a triple bottom line of "people, planet, and profit"), perhaps not as many of us are familiar with positive psychology. This movement is the study of human flourishing with a focus on the good or positive attributes of life and represents a shift in the field of psychology from focusing on why people are mentally ill to focusing on what makes people happy. Key lessons from the positive psychology movement are provided, including an action plan for implementation in the workplace. Section One ends with suggestions for overcoming impediments and criteria for choosing pathways.

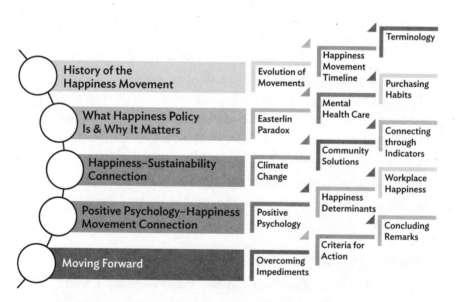

Figure I.1. Roadmap to Section One: The Landscape of the Happiness Movement.

Section Two of this handbook provides action plans that can be implemented sequentially or can be customized to fit unique circumstances. The section starts with a description of a happiness proclamation and how it has been used by various policymakers. A model proclamation is provided as well as a model press release. The next action plan presented explains two approaches to creating happiness roles and responsibilities, with descriptions of approaches taken by various governments, from Bhutan to the United Arab Emirates (UAE) to cities in the United States. A model job description is provided to support these roles. Engaging the community through social media, the convening of global or local councils, and working with populations through online

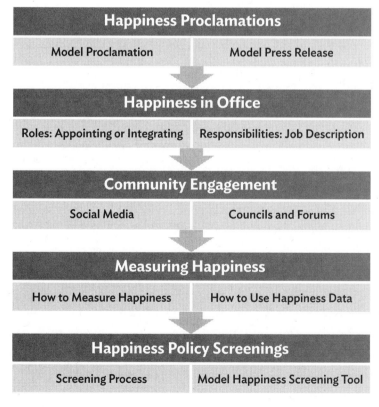

FIGURE I.2. Roadmap to Section Two: Action Plans for Happiness in Policy.

portals, town hall meetings, and world café style meetings is then explained. An action plan for policymakers' uses of social media platforms is provided. The action plan for measuring happiness includes an explanation of how to measure happiness with survey instruments and sampling procedures, along with an explanation about how to use happiness data. This action plan includes access to a subjective measure of happiness and well-being, the Happiness Index. Concluding Section Two is a happiness policy screening tool and instructions for using it.

It is our intent to help you gain understanding of what you need to take action. After reading *The Happiness Policy Handbook* you will be able to answer the following questions:

+ What is the happiness movement?
+ What is happiness policy?
+ What does happiness have to do with government?
+ What kinds of activities have governments undertaken in the happiness movement?
+ What are some of the impediments to happiness in public policy and what are some ways to overcome them?
+ What is a happiness proclamation?
+ What are three models for community engagement?
+ Can happiness be measured? If so, how?
+ What is the relationship between gross domestic product and happiness measurements?
+ How can happiness data be used?
+ How does one know if a happiness policy is working?

Extensive appendices are provided after Section Two. We have included a variety of policies and approaches, ranging from happiness proclamations and tools for measuring happiness, to community engagement methods. The Happiness Policy Screening Tool is also provided, along with examples of how to calibrate the tool in your own circumstances and how to interpret results.

The Landscape of the Happiness Movement

Learning the landscape of the happiness movement, like learning any landscape, includes understanding its history, its peaks and its valleys, where the possible impediments to progress lie, and which paths are best to undertake. This section is written in strokes broad enough to give a comprehensive portrait, and with enough detail that you can find a way to make meaningful progress in the happiness movement. It is intended as an overview and we hope inspires you to learn more.

1

Brief History of
the Happiness Movement

The origins of the happiness movement could be traced back to over 2,300 years ago, when Aristotle wrote in the Nicomachean Ethics, *happiness is the meaning and the purpose of life, the whole aim and end of human existence.* Aristotle's definition of happiness rests not on an emotional state but on what today is called *well-being.* The idea of well-being implies a state of flourishing with positive levels of health, economic prosperity (or not being impoverished), and social aspects. Happiness in Aristotelian terms includes living an ethical and virtuous life in relation to yourself and others. This same understanding of happiness seems to be what Thomas Jefferson meant when he said, "The care of human life and happiness, and not their destruction, is the only legitimate object of government."[1]

More recently, the happiness movement is based, in part, as a corrective to the unintended outcomes from the use of a measurement first employed during the Great Depression, and that later helped to gauge nations' progress towards economic recovery after World War II. This measurement is the gross domestic product (GDP). As mentioned earlier, this is the sum of all goods and services produced in a year within a country's borders (as a point of interest, Gross National Product [GNP] is the sum produced by citizens or corporations of a nation, regardless of the site of production). The originator of GDP, Simon Kuznets, cautioned the US Congress not to use GDP as a measurement to understand "the welfare of a nation."[2] The unintended consequences of a focus on economic production and its measurement have contributed to environmental degradation threatening the survival of many species including our own, social inequalities, and high levels of stress and unhappiness. An example is that economic value is created when natural resources are exploited, environments polluted, and clean up of pollution and contamination contributes to GDP. Nevertheless, GDP has become the predominant measurement of economic growth, which remains the predominant goal for most governments around the world.

Deeper Dive into
Essential Reading for the Happiness Movement

Key Books, Articles, Reports, or Videos

Essential reading for the happiness movement includes the *World Happiness Reports*, which rank countries and explore related issues, the *Global Happiness Policy Reports*, which focus on key policy topics, the *Stiglitz-Sen-Fitoussi Report*, which helped usher in the happiness movement, and the *BRAINPOoL Final Report*, which gives a snapshot of the happiness movement in 2014.

The *World Happiness Reports*, edited by John Helliwell, Richard Layard, and Jeffrey Sachs, have been issued every year since 2012 (with the exception of 2014) by the Sustainable Development Solutions Network. The first report was issued at the United Nation's High-Level Meeting: Well-Being and Happiness: Towards a New Economic Paradigm. Each report contains a ranking of countries based on satisfaction with life measured with the Cantril Ladder scale question, and an explanation of rankings based on six factors: (1) GDP per capita, (2) generosity, (3) healthy life expectancy, (4) perceived freedom to make life decisions, (5) social support, and (6) trust in government. Reports also contain analysis of factors and policies that contribute to happiness, such as mental health and family support, as well as discussions about data collection, definitions, and theoretical foundations for happiness (worldhappiness.report).

The *Global Happiness Policy Reports* are issued annually since 2018 at the Global Dialogue for Happiness in Dubai and are produced by the Global Happiness Council. They contain analysis of happiness policies by subject areas, ranging from data collection processes to educational programs, and city level programs, such as walkability and civic engagement through social media (happinesscouncil.org).

The *Report of the Commission on the Measurement of Economic Performance and Social Progress*, commonly called the *Stiglitz-Sen-Fitoussi Report*, has served as a pivotal influence in the happiness movement by pinpointing what is wrong with using GDP as the primary metric for policy. The report calls on governments to use wider measures of well-being. Flaws identified with using GDP as the primary measure of progress include discounting social inequality, detrimental effects on quality of life, and threats to sustainable development such that future generations will not be able to meet their basic needs (ec.europa.eu/eurostat/documents/118025/118123/Fitoussi +Commission+report).

The European Commission's project called Bringing Alternative Indicators into Policy (BRAINPOoL) concluded in 2014 with a report analyzing the state of the happiness movement. The report, *BRAINPOoL Final Report: Beyond GDP—From Measurement to Politics and Policy*, identified impediments to the happiness movement at that time, including confusion about terminology, lack of common agreement upon a happiness indicator or set of indicators, resource constraints to collecting data, lack of understanding about what happiness policy is or how to use data in relation to policy, and lack of cohesion between governmental departments in collecting and using happiness data or making policy decisions for happiness (cordis .europa.eu/project/rcn/100577/reporting/en).

The happiness movement in terms of government policies began a few years after the turn of the millennium. In 2008, the nation of Bhutan, situated north of India and to the east of Nepal, adopted a constitution that set the purpose of policy to promote the "condition that will enable the pursuit of Gross National Happiness."[3] Gross National Happiness (GNH), a term used in lieu of gross domestic product, is measured with a survey-based instrument and objective metrics that encompassed the aspects of community vitality, cultural diversity and resilience, ecological diversity and resilience, education, good governance, health, living standards, psychological well-being, and time use. Policies are promulgated and implemented for the explicit purpose of the happiness and well-being of people, with the understanding that ecological conservation, a strong cultural identity, sustainable economic activity, and good governance are central to happiness.[4] A Gross National Happiness Commission was formed to work with all governmental departments for the integration of happiness into all aspects of government and a GNH screening tool was created to assist in making decisions about policies and programs. This made international headlines and garnered much attention (both positive and negative).

On the heels of the Bhutanese government's adoption of happiness as its core purpose, international institutions and other governments took action. In 2009, the *Stiglitz-Sen-Fitoussi Report* was issued explaining the need for governments to use wider measures of well-being based on income equality and other inequalities.[5] In 2011, the Organisation for Economic Co-operation and Development (OECD), the organization that traditionally collects and reports GDP data for member nations, released a suggested wider measure of well-being, called the Better Life Index.[6] The OECD is comprised of thirty-six member countries, and its mission is to "promote policies that will improve the economic and social well-being of people around the world."[7] It is worth noting the countries comprising membership of the OECD: Australia, Austria, Belgium, Canada, Chile, Czech Republic, Denmark, Estonia, Finland, France, Germany, Greece, Hungary, Iceland, Ireland, Israel, Italy, Japan, Korea, Latvia, Lithuania, Luxembourg, Mexico, Netherlands, New Zealand, Norway, Poland, Portugal, Slovak Republic, Slovenia, Spain, Sweden, Switzerland, Turkey, United Kingdom, and the United States. It is clear that members include some of the most advanced countries in the world in terms of economic development, along with others in various stages of development. Additionally, they have cooperative relationships with some of the advanced developing countries of the world, such as Indonesia, South Africa, and the BRIC countries (Brazil, Russia, India, and China).

The United Kingdom began to measure happiness in 2011,[8] the same year the United Nations passed resolution 65/309 *Happiness: towards a holistic approach to development.*[9] In 2012, the first *World Happiness Report* was issued at the United Nations High-Level Meeting Well-being and Happiness: Defining a New Economic Paradigm.[10] In 2013, the OECD issued the *Guidelines for Measuring Subjective Well-being.*[11] In 2014, the European Union commission issued a report on the happiness and well-being movement, the *BRAINPOoL Final Report.*[12] One of the recommendations in the report was to use terms such as well-being in lieu of happiness in some political climates. By 2016, every European Union country was measuring happiness and well-being.[13] In 2017, a Minister of Happiness was appointed in the United Arab Emirates government and the first Global Dialogue for Happiness event was convened.[14] In 2018, the first *Global Happiness Policy Report* was issued.[15] Many other events, from conferences to courses, reports to resolutions, have occurred in the happiness movement and contributed to its momentum.

At the local level, many cities have joined the happiness movement. One of the first was in Brazil, in the state of Saõ Paulo, where academics collaborated with local schools and the mayor to gather happiness data through surveys, convene world café style meetings and work with the local government to implement interventions decided by the people surveyed. In 2010, the mayor along with the local health authority, the Victoria Foundation, and other stakeholders in Victoria, British Columbia, used a version of Bhutan's Gross National Happiness index to survey the population and hold town meetings about the results. In 2011, the Happiness Alliance, at that time a project of Sustainable Seattle,

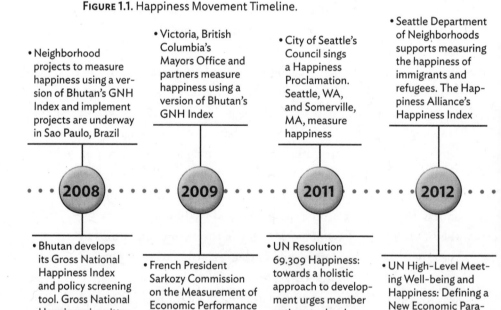

FIGURE 1.1. Happiness Movement Timeline.

• Neighborhood projects to measure happiness using a version of Bhutan's GNH Index and implement projects are underway in Sao Paulo, Brazil

• Victoria, British Columbia's Mayors Office and partners measure happiness using a version of Bhutan's GNH Index

• City of Seattle's Council sings a Happiness Proclamation. Seattle, WA, and Somerville, MA, measure happiness

• Seattle Department of Neighborhoods supports measuring the happiness of immigrants and refugees. The Happiness Alliance's Happiness Index

2008   **2009**   **2011**   **2012**

• Bhutan develops its Gross National Happiness Index and policy screening tool. Gross National Happiness is written into the constitution

• French President Sarkozy Commission on the Measurement of Economic Performance and Social Progress (The Stieglitz Report) calls for governments to use wiser measures of well-being

• UN Resolution 69.309 Happiness: towards a holistic approach to development urges member nations to develop wider measures of well-being
• United Kingdom Office of National Statistics begins to measure happiness

• UN High-Level Meeting Well-being and Happiness: Defining a New Economic Paradigm is held in NYC
• UN Resolution 66/281: International Day of Happiness is passed
• First World Happiness Report is issued

worked with the Seattle City Council to survey the population and provide an analysis of the data for budgeting decisions. Another effort was that of the mayor's office in Somerville, Massachusetts, to measure the happiness and well-being of its population. They used the data they gathered to support policy decisions. A year later, in 2012, Santa Monica, California, was awarded one million dollars from the Bloomberg Foundation to measure happiness and well-being. In 2015, Happy City, a nonprofit in Bristol, United Kingdom, began to measure the happiness of neighborhoods as well as the city at large. Numerous other governments and community organizers have also joined the happiness movement, many of them using the Happiness Alliance's happiness index. Figure 1.1 provides a view of the timeline of the happiness movement at the national and local levels.

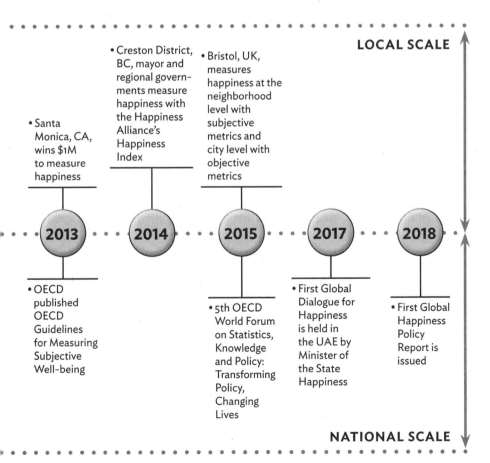

LOCAL SCALE

• Creston District, BC, mayor and regional governments measure happiness with the Happiness Alliance's Happiness Index

• Bristol, UK, measures happiness at the neighborhood level with subjective metrics and city level with objective metrics

• Santa Monica, CA, wins $1M to measure happiness

2013 ··· **2014** ··· **2015** ··· **2017** ··· **2018**

• OECD published OECD Guidelines for Measuring Subjective Well-being

• 5th OECD World Forum on Statistics, Knowledge and Policy: Transforming Policy, Changing Lives

• First Global Dialogue for Happiness is held in the UAE by Minister of the State Happiness

• First Global Happiness Policy Report is issued

NATIONAL SCALE

An Evolution of Sustainable Development: The Happiness Movement

In many aspects, the happiness movement extends the sustainability movement and helps move it forward, with a focus on human flourishing and societal well-being. The sustainability movement is generally considered to have begun in 1987, with the Brundtland Commission's report *Our Common Future* seen as a way of re-shaping the environmental movement for a broader focus. There were certainly earlier efforts to raise awareness of environmental issues, including Rachel Carson's seminal work, *Silent Spring*, in 1962. Today, the United Nations continues to use the term "sustainable development" broadly, and this is one reason that the UN High-Level Meeting Well-being and Happiness: Defining a New Economic Paradigm, was held under the umbrella of the UN's sustainable development arm. Nevertheless, over time, sustainability for many has come to be synonymous with environmentalism. While the sustainability movement has elicited very beneficial impacts and raised awareness, as evidenced by environmental protection laws worldwide, the popularity of businesses measuring and managing sustainability, and the creation of sustainability departments in governments, it often leaves out important aspects of economic equality, societal well-being, and personal happiness. The happiness movement can be thought of as an evolution of the sustainability movement, or as bringing it back to its original intent of encompassing economic, social, and environmental aspects, while expanding it to more thoroughly include personal aspects. Newer efforts to expand sustainability can be seen, for example, in the broader UN Sustainable Development Goals (which, by the way, include one goal on health and well-being).

A Few Words about Terminology

The happiness movement represents a wider understanding of individual and national well-being that includes satisfaction with life as well as the domains of community, culture, economy, envi-

FIGURE 1.2. Terms for Happiness.

ronment, government, human settlements, lifelong learning and education, physical and psychological health, social support, time balance, and work. This is the reason we often see the term well-being used synonymously with happiness.[16] The word happiness, in reference to the happiness movement, is often used synonymously with the terms well-being, quality of life, or better life. Another term that is used is "beyond GDP." Often happiness and well-being are used together. Figure 1.2 shows the common terms for happiness and some of the allied names.

Between 2011 and 2014, the European Commission's Bringing Alternative Indicators into Policy (BRAINPOoL) project studied the hurdles faced by the happiness movement through work done by governments to adopt wider measures of well-being in lieu of GDP. One of the conclusions was that terminology could act as an impediment when the term happiness is used. It is important to assess the circumstances and political climate of a given area before settling on a word. One of the benefits of the term happiness is that it is attractive to people and to the media. One of the drawbacks is that it can be seen as improper or not serious enough for government. Regardless of terminology, a step that should not be overlooked is educating the public, media, and colleagues about the definition of happiness, well-being, quality of life, better life, beyond GDP, or other terms.

2

What Happiness Policy Is
and Why It Matters

Happiness policies are different from other policies because they are promulgated with the primary aim of securing the happiness of people. Examples of happiness policies can be found in the *World Happiness Reports*, *Global Happiness Policy Report*, *Well-Being for Public Policy*, and other relevant publications. In addition, many policies already in place both secure people's opportunities to pursue their happiness and enhance their well-being but have not been evaluated with happiness measurements. Likewise, there are examples of policies, programs, and projects that have been evaluated with happiness, well-being, or quality of life data but have not been adopted widely.

Happiness and well-being policy encompasses feelings of joy and satisfaction with life, ecological and human health, wealth and prosperity, and many other factors because it is founded on an understanding that personal happiness and well-being are intrinsically linked to the sustainability of our planet, health of economies, and well-being of society. Happiness policy encompasses economic, social, and environmental policy. It also encompasses aspects of community, culture, education, governance, health, human settlements, psychological well-being, time balance, and work, as well as affect (positive and negative feelings) and satisfaction with life. It is policy that is connected to all aspects of human existence, because individual and collective happiness and well-being are connected to all aspects of human existence.

It is this notion of connectedness that makes a difference in people's lives. An allied discipline, community development, is built on this foundation of connectedness, belonging, and interaction in places where we live. Community development, whether as a concept, goal, process, or outcome is most simply about making things better for people where they live.[1] Community development is intricately related to community well-being, which refers to how well a community is doing collectively.[2] There are many points of intersectionality between community development, community well-being, sustainability, and happiness. It continues to emerge as a varied and beneficial area of research and practice around the globe.

Because happiness policy is comprehensive, broadly encompassing and connected to all aspects of people's happiness, societal well-being, and planetary sustainability, it is guided by goals for economic equality, social justice, human rights, nature's rights, sustainable production and consumption, good governance, human flourishing, ecosystem health, and many other aspects of well-being for human and other life forms.

One way to define happiness policy is through *domains*, also called life circumstances, and the aspects within domains that are measured with happiness indicators. These domains and aspects are:

- Psychological well-being, which includes affect (positive and negative feelings), flourishing, mental illness and health, and satisfaction with life.
- Community, which includes belonging, crime and safety, development approaches, discrimination, generosity, and social support.
- Culture, which includes cultural activities, cultural identity, and values.
- Economy, which includes economic equity and equality, food, housing, jobs, consumption and production, business and entrepreneurship, income and innovation.

+ Education and lifelong learning, which includes both formal education and informal education.
+ Environment, which includes access to nature, air, biodiversity, climate change, natural resources, soil, and water.
+ Governance, which includes confidence, engagement, human rights, participation, and trust.
+ Health, which includes care, illness, habits, healthy life expectancy, and sense of energy.
+ Time balance, which includes feeling rushed, enjoying the things one does, and leisure time.
+ Work, which includes autonomy, fair pay, meaningful work, productivity, and satisfaction with work, and work–life balance.

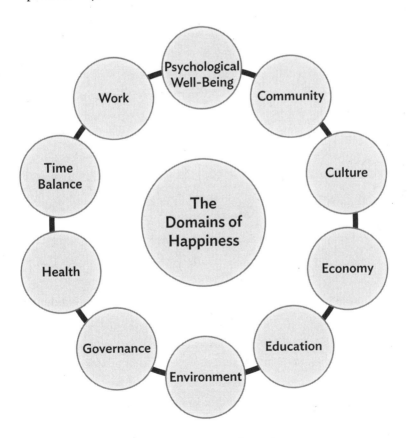

FIGURE 2.1. The Domains of Happiness.

In other words, these domains or life circumstances encompass the dimensions and aspects of the lives we live, and ways we interact with each other, all living things, and our places on earth. Figure 2.1 provides an illustration of these domains of happiness.

Deeper Dive into Happiness Policy

Understand more about why happiness policy matters by watching a few films.

There is a straightforward answer to the question of why happiness policy matters in the *Global Happiness Policy Report 2018*:

"...measures of subjective well-being, and especially of life evaluations, provide an overall indicator of the quality of life. Having such an umbrella measure of well-being makes it possible to evaluate and compare the economic and social consequences of policies on a consistent basis." (*Global Happiness Report 2018*, p. 13)

In other words, happiness policy can make a difference in communities, regions, and countries. It is this potential, and its actualization, that make happiness policies important to consider.

You can consider the impacts of changes on cultures by watching *Happiness*, a 2013 film by Thomas Balmes. It is a documentary about Bhutan and the incursion of technology, and what changes they experience as a result. See a link and commentary via the Public Broadcasting Service (PBS) at pbs .org/independentlens/blog/pursuit-happiness-thomas-balmes/. A thought-provoking piece, it reminds of us of other considerations around consumerism and its impacts on economies and societies. Annie Leonard, a filmmaker who is an advocate for more sustainable living (and current Executive Director of Greenpeace USA), has a series of short movies about the impacts of high levels of consumerism. Her classic 2011 film, *The Story of Stuff*, is a gateway to opening conversations around consumerism and its impacts on affect and well-being. See her website with links to each film: storyofstuff.org/movies/.

The film *Happy*, written and directed by Roco Belic (2011), gives the rational for the happiness movement though a series of personal stories punctuated by facts and theories from experts. It can be used to educate and inspire anyone, including those with little knowledge of the happiness movement, in a fun and amusing way. The film can be streamed from various entertainment sites or rented online on The Happy Movie website at thehappymovie.com.

A core tenet of this handbook is that the primary purpose of government is to secure equal opportunities for people to pursue happiness. Policymakers worldwide are starting to recognize that governments today are failing in too many ways and for too many people because of over-reliance on metrics, goals, and policies for economic growth to the exclusion of other types of development. They are seeing that using gross domestic product (GDP) as the predominant metric to guide policy can result in economic inequality, environmental degradation, and social injustice. While unprecedented growth and development has occurred since GDP was chosen as a major index, there have often been undesirable and unintended consequences of a focus that favors economics over other dimensions. Policymakers are seeing that economic growth disconnected from social good and environmental sustainability has also led to increasing gaps between the wealthy and poor, use of natural resources outpacing renewal rates, and climate change. Longitudinal research findings reveal that in a stable economy, once people have an income of between US$35,000 and $75,000 annually, increases in income do not make people happier.[3] Despite these findings, there continue to be widening gaps in income inequality, sometimes as a result of economic policy.

While there have been significant efforts to produce evidence that specific policies enhance happiness, the field is new enough that more evidence is still very much needed. A one-size-fits-all policy does not exist that will increase happiness for every person. Instead, to understand what policies will increase happiness it is important to understand in what domains people perceive themselves to be thriving and where they perceive themselves to be hurting. To understand whether a policy once implemented has increased happiness and well-being, it is important to have a baseline, and to measure its impact compared to the baseline. This can be done with happiness measurements, which are covered in the second section of this handbook. In Appendix A: Concept Menu of Happiness Policies, ideas are listed for happiness policies organized by the various domains of happiness.

Happiness Policy Makes Economic Sense

The happiness movement has its roots in the field of economics, and many of its leaders are economists. Joseph Stiglitz, Amartya Sen, and Jean-Paul Fitoussi, authors of the *Stiglitz-Sen-Fitoussi Report*, are economists. The three editors (and authors of many chapters) of the *World Happiness Reports*, John Helliwell, Richard Layard, and Jeffrey Sachs, are also economists. The OECD, which issued the *Guidelines for Measuring Subjective Well-being* and the *Better Life Index*, was formed with the purpose of economic cooperation and development (hence its name). Other prominent leaders, including Gus O'Donnell and Alan Krueger, are also economists. Psychologist Daniel Kahneman won the Nobel prize in economics for his work investigating the use of affect (feelings) and satisfaction scales to understand decision making, thereby expanding economists' understanding of utility and decision making.

With so many economists leading the happiness movement, the question of the economic advantages of happiness policy has not gone unanswered. Chapter Three of the *Global Happiness Policy Report*, "Mental Illness Destroys Happiness and Is Costless to Treat," asks every nation to provide mental health care services to their populations, citing the costs as .01 percent of GDP at the onset and net negative over time. Chapter Four of the *World Happiness Report 2013*, "The Objective Benefits of Subjective Well-Being," identifies how employment, consumption, and savings policies guided by the goal of people's happiness can yield wide and more sustainable economic benefits. The Legatum Institute's *Wellbeing and Policy* report proposes a revamping of cost-benefit analysis for public policy, introducing satisfaction with life into the equation.[4] Individual studies of the economic benefits of happiness, well-being, and sustainable development policies are numerous. However, the absence of any use of happiness metrics by governments to measure the performance of such policies may be one reason that so few of these studies are known.

Deeper Dive into Happiness Policy and Economics

Learn more about the relationships between happiness policy and economics.

There are many aspects to consider when thinking about happiness policy and economics, not least of which is to gauge the impact of change on local areas as well as regional and national economies. With rapid industrialization across the globe, as well as changes impacting how and where products are made and services provided, it is key to look at how these relationships impact happiness.

There are so many ways to explore economics in local and regional economies. One of our favorites is via the film, *The Economics of Happiness*. This was made by the nonprofit group, Local Futures, whose mission is to "renew ecological, social and spiritual well-being by promoting a systemic shift towards economic localization" (see their website localfutures.org). While the film does not go into too many specific economic concepts, it illustrates the impact of economics on local happiness. A short version can be accessed via: localfutures.org/programs /the-economics-of-happiness/the-film/.

There are other resources too for learning more about happiness and economics, particularly in the context of local communities. A group formed several years ago, the Business Alliance for Local Living Economies (BALLE), meets periodically to engage people across a spectrum of interests in helping their communities and region thrive with locally-focused economies. In turn, these areas build stronger social and cultural relationships and support environmental health with local food systems or sourcing locally and regionally. More information about BALLE can be found at bealocalist.org/.

Researchers have demonstrated some important lessons for happiness that have an impact on all people, regardless of whether any one person is interested in promoting the happiness of other people or even their own. Each of these lessons has policy implications. A few are outlined below.

Easterlin Paradox

Once a person's income is adequate to meet their material needs, increases in income bring increasingly marginal increases in happiness, so that to increase happiness just a small amount after a certain level would entail very large income gains. This is called the Easterlin Paradox,[5] after Richard Easterlin, the economist who first formulated it. After a certain income level, people gain much greater happiness levels from rewarding jobs, healthy and stable relationships, and strong families. The policy implications are that resources should be focused on ensuring everyone has an opportunity to earn adequate income to meet their material needs, but after this point, resources are better expended to provide rewarding jobs, and to encourage strong and healthy relationships and families.

Income Inequality

Large income and wealth gaps, defined in terms of Gini coefficients, have a deleterious effect on the happiness and well-being of everybody, even the very wealthy. The Gini coefficient was developed in 1912 by Corrado Gini, an Italian statistician and sociologist, to measure inequality, and is still used by governments and international institutions.[6] Harmful effects of high levels of inequality (as indicated by high Gini coefficients) extend from many aspects of physical health to psychological well-being.[7] The policy implications concern lowering or managing Gini coefficients through employment, tax, housing, food, and health policies in areas where these coefficients are high.

Mental Health Care

Mental illness carries a stigma in many cultures that acts as a barrier to receiving appropriate mental health care. However, mental illness is experienced by almost every person at some point in their lives and often has lasting detrimental impacts on physical health.[8] It also leads to antisocial behaviors, decreases in social connection, feelings of loneliness (which in turn often lead to increased consumption of material goods), and lower levels of happiness and satisfaction with life. Policy implications point to the destigmatization of mental illness, reprioritization of mental health care, and provision of mental health care.

Purchasing Habits

Spending disposable income yields a hierarchy of happiness benefits: the shortest-term happiness impact comes from buying material goods. A longer-lasting happiness benefit comes from buying experiences.[9] The longest-lasting happiness benefit comes from donating money to charitable causes.[10] Purchasing habits have other and even longer-lasting impacts on happiness when looking to their effect on the environment as the source sustaining human life and capacity for well-being. About seventy percent of the GDP in the US is driven by consumer spending.[11] The Bureau of Economic Analysis (2016) states that it is the "primary engine that drives future economic growth."[12] The reliance on consumer spending to foster economic growth through conscious plans developed in the 1950s, exemplified by this statement made by Victor Lebow:

> Our enormously productive economy demands that we make consumption our way of life, that we convert the buying and use of goods into rituals, that we seek our spiritual satisfaction and our ego satisfaction in consumption. We need things consumed, burned up, worn out, replaced and discarded at an ever-increasing rate.[13]

There is a real and significant cost to consuming without regard for our environment that threatens human well-being on multiple levels.[14] Policy implications include encouraging pro-social purchasing patterns and ensuring sustainable production practices for all aspects of production from extraction of natural resources to transportation, packaging, end of use, or life practices.

3

The Happiness–Sustainability Connection

Climate Change

Happiness policy has the potential to make significant impacts regarding the environment. There is overwhelming evidence that the impact of climate change on our ecosystems, on the health of all aspects of our planet from our oceans to all living species requires our urgent attention. The United Nations, in its *UN Climate Change Annual Report 2017* states:

> Climate change is the defining challenge of our time, yet it is still accelerating faster than our efforts to address it. Atmospheric levels of carbon dioxide are higher than they have been for 800,000 years, and they are increasing. So, too, are the catastrophic effects of our warming planet—extreme storms, droughts, fires, floods, melting ice and rising sea levels.[1]

Numerous mainstream reports written for policymakers have loudly and clearly sounded the warnings on why we cannot continue behaving the way we do. In 2018, the Intergovernmental Panel on Climate Change (IPCC) *Special Report on Global Warming 2018* set a limit of ten years before the impacts of the warming of the planet, ranging from catastrophic flooding, droughts, forest fires, melting sea ice, and rising sea levels, were felt by all nations and peoples of the world. In 2018, the IPCC's *Summary for Policymakers Report* provided robust and concise data for use by policymakers that points the way for public policy decisions.[2]

The American National Aeronautics and Space Administration (NASA) also provides a long list of concrete evidence on climate change that ranges from tracking global temperature rise, warming oceans, shrinking ice sheets, glacial retreat, decreased snow cover, sea level rise, declining Arctic sea ice, extreme weather events, and ocean acidification on a dedicated website at climate.nasa.gov /evidence.

The Local–Global Connection: Community Solutions to Sustainable Development

As we are more connected across the world than ever, it is critical that local communities engage in discussion around happiness and sustainability. It is often at the local level that we actualize what sustainability means, whether, for example, as a local policy, program, or ethos about conservation. In some cases, communities have embarked on the design of policies to directly address their concerns about environmental quality, or to foster a locally-focused economy to buffer against global-level changes in industry structure. It is even more critical now, as changes across the world impact climate, economy, and society, that local communities understand, identify, gauge, and craft responses to issues affecting their members' ability to thrive and pursue happiness.

Connecting Sustainable Development to Happiness Through Indicators

As communities grapple with the impacts of climate change, policymakers are presented with increasing opportunities to tie in happiness indicators to the environment to help shape the direction of public policy. Using these indicators for gauging progress towards policy goals can serve as a beneficial tool for fostering understanding and raising awareness. Oftentimes these indicators are constructed by citizens and advocates in their communities to express their own priorities (these could be, for example, concern with environmental quality or prevalent health issues, etc.).[3]

For the most part sustainability indicators have been objective, capturing the status of states such as the degree of biodiversity, water quality, or poverty rates. These states can be seen and measured. There are several reasons for this. One is that only recently have subjective metrics been considered reliable for policymakers, researchers, and others. Another is because of the emphasis on the capabilities approach, which assumes that people must have certain objectively measurable needs met before they can be happy. While there is some truth to this, the use of subjective metrics has also revealed that people can be happy even when they do not meet certain objective criteria for happiness, such as income levels.[4] Exploring why people are satisfied with life and happy, when objectively indicators suggest they should be miserable, has the potential to reveal important solutions to people's happiness and the sustainability of the planet.

Deeper Dive into the Happiness and Sustainability Connection

Read and hear about how communities are meeting the goals of well-being and sustainability in the state of Vermont, how the nation of Bhutan is affecting ecological and social health with its Gross National Happiness philosophy, listen to a talk about the context and complexities of sustaining human life on our planet, and gain perspective on happiness metrics.

Read about models, policies, and programs in the state of Vermont that achieved the combined goals of community cohesion, ecological and just economies, and environmental sustainability. Sample programs and policies include the institution of an energy efficiency utility company, Efficiency Vermont, that worked with customers to reduce energy use, greenhouse gas emissions, and costs to consumers while creating green jobs;

the restoration of an informal and illegal dumping ground into hiking trails, wetland, and farms with the capacity to grow ten percent of the local food supply in a project called Intervale; and a computer literacy and microfinance program that included psychological counseling and support for refugees. See *Sustainable Communities: Creating a Durable Local Economy* by Rhonda Phillips, Bruce Seifer, and Ed Antczak (Routledge, 2014).

Hear about how Bhutan is achieving carbon neutrality as part of Gross National Happiness enshrined in its constitution through generating green energy, strengthening the national culture, developing processes to foster trust in government, and preserving biodiversity through protection of forests in Prime Minister of Bhutan Tshering Tobgay's TED Talk, "This country isn't just carbon neutral—it's carbon negative" at ted .com/talks/tshering_tobgay_this_country_isn_t_just_carbon _neutral_it_s_carbon_negative?language=en and un-denial .com/2018/04/29/by-nate-hagens-contrasts-and-coninuums -of-the-human-predicament/.

Learn about issues of ecological sustainability in the context of human evolution, psychology, and culture, and the implications for personal choices, public policies, and social change, concluding with three solutions: (1) how to educate and inspirit small groups of change makers, (2) how to empower individuals to make choices that lead to psychological flourishing, and (3) how to change the culture through conversations based on the reality of today's social, economic, and ecological state, in a talk by Nate Hagens given on Earth Day at un-denial.com/2018 /04/29/by-nate-hagens-contrasts-and-continuums-of-the -human-predicament.

Gain perspective on the connections between sustainable development and happiness metrics through an analysis of the Sustainable Development Goals (SDG) indicators in comparison to an aggregate of happiness indices that yields an analysis of gaps in the SDG indicator scheme and identification of specific happiness indicators to fill those gaps. Download the article *Bridging the Gap between the Sustainable Development Goals and Happiness Metrics* by Leire Iriarte and Laura Musikanski in *International Journal of Community Well-being* at link.springer.com/journal/42413/1/1.

4

Connections between
Positive Psychology and the
Happiness Movement

The Positive Psychology Movement

Positive psychology is an evolution in the field of psychology, where until recently the predominant focus has been on mental illness instead of mental wellness. This revolutionary approach to understanding human psychology from a perspective of what is needed for mental health instead of what causes mental illness was first conceived by Abraham Maslow, who is best known for articulating the Maslow Hierarchy of Needs. Maslow's concept of a hierarchy of needs and his theory that a modicum of lower level needs must be met before higher needs can be fulfilled is widely accepted.[1] The term "positive psychology" was coined and the concept made popular under the leadership of Martin Seligman and Mihaly Csikszentmihalyi in 1998.[2]

Psychologists Seligman and Csikszentmihalyi ushered in a greater focus on what makes us happy and how to develop our capacity for well-being. A field of positive psychology was developed under Seligman's leadership that has yielded an abundance of scientific findings that point the way for policymakers. This line of inquiry has been picked up by researchers in other disciplines. In the fields of economics, philosophy, the sciences, and other areas, important work is being done that can aid policymakers in determining which policies to consider for securing the happiness of their citizenry.

FIGURE 4.1. Maslow's Hierarchy of Needs.
Credit: Created by authors based on Maslow's Hierarchy of Needs.

Happiness Determinants

Explorations into the determinants of happiness by researchers including Jan-Emmanuel De Neve and Sonja Lyubomirsky have revealed important information for policymakers and others (see Deeper Dive for more information).

Happiness determinants generally fall into three categories: genetics, life circumstances, and mental processes. Life conditions and mental processes account for at least half of a person's happiness.[3] Life circumstances include the economic, social, cultural, and ecological environments. This is relevant for policymakers because it means that *the circumstances of life can be changed to ensure people have opportunities to pursue happiness.* There is much to draw on from the field of positive psychology for the formation of public policy.

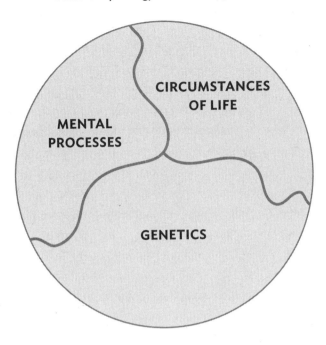

Figure 4.2. Happiness Determinants.

Deeper Dive into the Positive Psychology and Happiness Movement Connection

Gain a practical understanding of positive psychology by reading two of its seminal books, learn why a Nobel Prize in Economics was awarded to a psychologist and what the main hurdles are to applying happiness metrics to policy, and read about how leading positive psychologists see the connection between personal happiness and the happiness movement.

Two books that help to understand the practical and personal applications of positive psychology are *The How of Happiness: A New Approach to Getting the Life You Want* (Penguin Books, 2007) by Sonja Lyubomirsky and *Flourish: A Visionary New Understanding of Happiness and Well-being* (Atria Books, 2012) by Martin Seligman. With *The How of Happiness*, Lyubomirsky brought the concept of determinants of happiness (genetics, social conditions, and mental habits) into popular focus, and laid out twelve activities based on positive psychology research findings extending from practicing gratitude and generosity to fostering relationships and avoiding social comparisons. *Flourish* explains Seligman's concept PERMA, whereby practices for developing greater experiences of positive emotions, deeper engagement, stronger relationships, a sense of meaning, and accomplishment are provided.

In 2002, Daniel Kahneman, a psychologist, won a Nobel Prize in Economics for challenging the fundamental idea behind economic theory that decisions are made on a rational basis with evidence that decisions are made based on remembered experience and other aspects of human psychology. This is important for policymakers because how people remember their experiences influences their decisions about life, from where they live to the jobs they take, family choices, and voting patterns. Policy implications of his research include the formation of behavioral insights (also called nudging) departments in governments. Watch Kahneman's Ted Talk The riddle of experience vs. memory at ted.com/talks/daniel_kahneman_the _riddle_of_experience_vs_memory?language=en

Carol Graham was among the earliest scholars to see the connections between happiness research, happiness metrics, and public policy, and to pinpoint issues policymakers must consider when using happiness metrics. These include the definition of happiness, the theoretical basis for happiness, how happiness is measured, the human capacity for adaptation (which allows for people to be happy in seemingly unhappy situations), and the determination of a basis for policy priorities. *The Pursuit of Happiness: An Economy of Well-Being* (Brookings Institution Press, 2011).

Through their scholarship, Ed Diener, known as "Dr. Happiness," and Martin Seligman have contributed together and separately to connecting research findings in the positive psychology field to the happiness movement in terms of the development of happiness and well-being indicators' policy implications. The development and use of well-being metrics by government and promulgation of policy that supports social connectiveness, relationships, and community are common themes in their work. Read their early work *Beyond Money: Towards an Economy of Well-Being*, published in *Psychological Science in the Public Interest* at labs.psychology.illinois.edu /~ediener/Documents/Diener-Seligman_2004.pdf

Workplace Happiness

There is also much to draw on from positive psychology for the workplace. Happiness science reveals that happy people are more successful in their endeavors and in their relationships.[4] Moreover, when employees are able to connect their own purpose to the purpose of their work, they are more engaged and effective.[5]

Workplace happiness comes in many forms. Appendix B: Happiness Lessons for the Workplace, presents tools for applying important lessons from positive psychology in the workplace. There are many different ways to increase happiness in the workplace, from the practices listed in Appendix B to others such as flex-time, job sharing, gym membership, and on-site child care. The *World Happiness Report* for 2013 identifies some workplace policies in Chapter Four, entitled "Restoring Virtue Ethics in the Quest for Happiness," as does Chapter Five of the *Global Happiness Policy Report* entitled "Work and Well-being: A Global Perspective," as well as many other publications. Indeed, even the venerable *Harvard Business Review* got on board with an entire issue dedicated to happiness a few years ago!

5

Moving Forward

Overcoming Impediments, Choosing Pathways

The pathway from an idea of happiness policy to its enactment can be simple and direct, or complicated and long. More often than not, enacting policy requires patience and a great deal of perseverance to overcome obstacles and inertia.

Every government, country, and culture have their own unique circumstances, requirements, and decision-making procedures that determine the process and outcome of an endeavor. In some governments, when decision-making power is relatively localized and there is leadership support, a relatively straightforward approach can be successful. Governments with multiple branches of leadership, bicameral legislatures, or parliaments are likely to present a more complicated and lengthy process.

In any government, it is important to allocate resources to build awareness, cohesion, and commitment to make change happen. There are many channels that can be employed for developing, publicizing, gaining support, and getting a proposal to the enactment stage. Some are discussed in Chapter Six, in the section about community engagement and proclamations. Almost always several of the channels will be involved, either sequentially or concurrently. Other channels include activism, analyses by respected experts, charrettes (focused meetings for planning, design, and analysis), educational systems, legislature negotiations, lobbying, political caucuses, social and professional organizations, and town meetings.

There has to be willingness, and willpower, for a government to make changes. When we think about managing change, it often seems that it requires a good deal of focused attention to encourage policymakers to push forward. In some cases, the policymakers themselves are advocating for the desired changes, at other times, much activity by others is needed and then government follows. When we look at a variety of innovative or progressive programs that have been adopted by governments, it is sometimes the case that they put the policies in place only after concentrated attention and interest generated by citizen activist groups or others advocating for the desired change. One noteworthy example of this is when citizens were alarmed by the die-off of wild salmon in the Seattle, Washington, area. They formed an advocacy group, Sustainable Seattle, that developed a system of indicators. The local government responded by implementing policies aimed at improving environmental quality. The salmon were a sign that something was amiss in the natural system. The residents of the area focused their attention on the interconnected nature of the systems that was causing the salmon die offs, leading to the first set of sustainability indicators issued by a community. This effort eventually resulted in positive changes in governmental policy. Sustainable Seattle's work served to inspire myriad other community and advisory groups, and local and regional governments to adopt their own indicators and policies to support sustainability.

Connecting to Community

Community is essentially people living together in a place. Community can also be defined through interests. Communities are indeed complex by their very nature and represent a full range of interaction and relational effects. We are social by nature and the need to interact with others is hardwired into our brains. The role

Deeper Dive into Community Organizing

Gain an understanding of ways to bring about change in the political landscape for community organizers and others seeking to work with policymakers.

When working to make change in a community as a community organizer, whether it is at the local, state/provincial, or national level, you need to build momentum. This includes, as noted, building awareness, educating both policymakers and constituents, finding places where cooperation is possible, and exploring whether resources are available. There are numerous ways to raise the profile of an issue with decision makers but the real test of whether or not you can influence change is in the capacity of you and your organization to apply and sustain pressure. It is not good enough to just identify the problem. It is essential to plan and build a campaign that is sustainable.

One of the ways to do this is through lobbying. Although the notion of lobbying has had some bad press, in its purest form lobbying is about informing decision makers, presenting alternatives to a problem or issue, and attempting to make change. It is a form of advocacy and influence. It is critical for citizens to understand that they have the ability and the power to shape policy. There are a number of resources outlining how to lobby and the National Trust for Historic Preservation's Preservation Leadership Forum on lobbying techniques is just one: forum. savingplaces.org/learn/fundamentals/advocacy/lobbying101 /lobbying-techniques.

E-petitions are another way to draw attention to an issue, and, depending on the jurisdiction, to elicit a response from the government. Many governments have the capacity for

e-petitions and Canada's House of Common's webpage
E-petitions is a good example: petitions.ourcommons.ca/en
/Home/Index. E-petitions can give people seeking change
a platform to raise the profile of their issue and to influence
decision makers. However, they are only one tool and cannot be
used as a standalone measure, but rather as part of a comprehensive communication package to garner attention.

Jeremy Heiman's post "How to build a successful movement in 4 easy steps," about his 2014 TED talk demonstrates
how to build a successful movement in today's much more
complicated climate of technology. The four steps are to work
with "connected connectors," develop a strong brand, make it
easy for people to participate, and help followers become leaders in the effort. He uses examples from both the corporate and
the social movement world to show how these techniques may
be used. Read the article and watch the TED talk at ideas.ted
.com/how-to-build-a-successful-movement-in-4-steps.

The American Civil Liberties Union (ACLU) used an
innovative approach with a humorous video, My Big Gay (Il)
legal Wedding, in its campaign to raise awareness about same
sex marriage laws. See the video at aclu.org/video/my-big-gay
-illegal-wedding-tim-gunn.

A different approach to making change in communities
is encapsulated in Asset Based Community Development
(ABCD). The notion is that the community has resources and
skills to make change and that successful change will build
on these assets. The ABCD Toolkit can be downloaded at
resources.depaul.edu/abcd-institute/resources/Documents
/WhatisAssetBasedCommunityDevelopment.pdf.

of happiness can be felt and seen within communities. You know it when you are in a place that is connected and moving forward with ideas and actions that enable it to be attractive, supportive, and enabling.

There is a chapter in the *Global Happiness Policy Report 2018* on happy cities. It is worth reading, particularly if you are interested in connecting to your community more deeply. They remind us in this chapter that the "spirit" of a community or place is vitally important. We believe it directly impacts the ability to define and implement happiness policies successfully. As pointed out, Plato long ago asserted that a community or city is what it is because the citizens are what they are. An observation from over two thousand years ago that holds as true today as then. We are what we make our communities to be, and taking explicit action to embody happiness and the spirit of a place can be very effective.

Deeper Dive into Community Connections

Read about community in terms of
overall well-being, and how to engage community.

A sense of solidarity and bonding, as well as acting collectively, are aspects of community. In other words, community can be identified when people live, work, and take action together in the place they live (or in some cases, in virtual communities or communities of interest instead of a geographical space). For policy, though, we usually talk about communities of place where local and regional government has oversight for policy design and implementation. If you are interested in learning more about communities of place, a textbook that is used in courses is *Introduction to Community Development*, 2nd edition, edited by Rhonda Phillips and Robert Pittman (Routledge, 2014).

Community refers to the collective, and in the case of community well-being, implies how we understand community and how we approach fulfilling the needs and desires of its members. Community is a wide-ranging umbrella, or concept, that encompasses many different elements in a collective and what influences its well-being. These could be economic, social, environmental, political, and cultural dimensions. How decisions are made, who governs, and how a community operates also influence the well-being of a community. As HeeKyung Sung and Rhonda Phillips explain in their 2018 article, "Indicators and Community Well-Being: Exploring a Relational Framework":

> The very concept of community well-being varies depending on whom is asked, community conditions and changes, how community itself is defined, and the nature of well-being—whether it is assumed to be more theoretical or applied. It can be thought of as an overarching umbrella, bringing together many aspects that can influence well-being of the collective. At the same time, how are these aspects decided upon and are there enough commonalities that guidance can be offered? All the above, and more, complicate the picture for communities and identification and measurement of their well-being.

See a collection of articles on community well-being in the newly established International Journal of Community Well-Being *(downloads are free for articles published in 2019 and 2020 at link.springer.com/journal/42413/1/1).*

There are many ways to engage members of a community, or to attract more members to a community. These community participation methods are based on a foundational principle that participation is essential for providing insights and opinions, as well as participating in decision making. In a democracy, it is particularly important that community members engage and participate. There are many resources available for learning more about how to engage community in processes and decision making, as well as mobilizing for impact. A resource for this includes the government of New Zealand's "Community led development tools and resources" at communitymatters .govt.nz/community-led-development-tools-and-resources-2/. This includes participation methods as well as learning about community as a whole.

Criteria for Taking Action

The next section presents action plans for integrating happiness into government. However, how does one determine when it is wise to take action? Appendix C: Strategy Resources presents several perspectives for organizing a change campaign to help gauge the right time to take action. Below is a proposed set of criteria that can help determine which plan of action would be most beneficial towards the goal of making happiness the purpose of government:

Awareness: Is there a general awareness of the happiness movement or an openness to new ideas in government and in society? If not, what are the avenues for building awareness and are there resources and people who can help build it?

Knowledge: Is there sufficient knowledge about the tenets of the happiness movement, the key findings of happiness science, and the important publications and events in the happiness movement for policymakers and government staff to implement the action plans wisely? If not, is it possible to educate people, host events, or ensure key people participate in events to gain knowledge? Is there sufficient awareness of the tangible benefits in implementing policies that promote and support happiness?

Cooperation: Will other policymakers, governmental staff, and other stakeholders cooperate with the process and institutional changes required? If not, what would be necessary for them to cooperate? Is it possible to use existing structures, such as political parties and community-based organizations, to inform, educate, and work towards cooperative change?

Resources: Are there sufficient resources available for implementation and continuity? Will institutional resources be allocated, including people's time, venues, and funding for implementation?

Concluding Remarks on the Happiness Movement

The happiness movement is at once a new paradigm and as old as history. In the sense that it is old, happiness is a basic drive of human existence, and the purpose of all we do, from governing ourselves to living daily life. We see traces of the old nature of the happiness movement in ancient philosophers' writings and various nations' constitutional documents. In the sense that it is new, it represents possibilities for governments and policymakers to take a leadership role from local to international levels. The science, literature, and development of happiness policy is not so new that there is little to draw from, but new enough that contributions can have a significant impact for populations and nations. It is the authors' hope that this book inspires and empowers current and future policymakers to contribute to a paradigmatic shift whereby happiness policy is the norm.

Happiness Action Plans for Policymakers

This section presents five action plans with resources and tools for implementing them. These action plans can be undertaken sequentially or individually. The tools and resources that are provided may be adopted in full or adapted to fit your circumstances.

6

Action Plan:
Happiness Proclamations

One of the first steps a policymaker can take to join the happiness movement is to issue a proclamation. A proclamation is a public announcement and is not legally binding. It does not promise or contract to do anything. A proclamation by a governmental body or policymakers denotes gravity and can be used to elevate the importance of an issue and raise awareness. It can also be a way to publicize plans and encourage engagement.

Media coverage often occurs with a happiness proclamation. The media is one conduit for educating the public about what government is doing, the impact it will have on them, and how they can participate. When making a happiness proclamation, it is important to educate the media about the concept of happiness and the government's plans.

Educating the media takes many forms. One is the proclamation itself. The proclamation should include a definition of happiness in broad terms. In the model proclamation included in Appendix D: The Happiness Proclamation, happiness is defined broadly to include feelings and satisfaction with life as well as the conditions of life ranging from the economy to social support and work. It should also include the basis for the proclamation by setting the historical context and by giving citations to background documents. The model proclamation includes a reference to the United Nations resolution 69/305. This can be replaced with a reference to a neighboring city, state, or country, or to other important documents supporting the happiness movement, such as the *World Happiness Reports*, the *Stiglitz-Sen-Fitoussi Report*, and many others. A proclamation should clearly state that the role of government is not to force people to take specific actions. It should also clarify that the role of government is to create the circumstances that allow each person to pursue happiness per their unique definition (within the limits of the law). A proclamation can also be used to outline the actions the government intends to take, such as exploring happiness and well-being metrics as outlined in the model proclamation and suggesting approaches for public participation. When the media is well educated, upon the release of a proclamation headlines will often read something along the lines of "Taking Happiness Seriously." The model proclamation in Appendix D provides a format for such proclamations.

POLICY HIGHLIGHT

How Can Governments Raise People's Happiness?

by Martine Durand

People's happiness today depends on their wider well-being—an array of life circumstances and living conditions that make life good and enable people to live the lives they have reason to value (see OECD Framework below). Sustaining that happiness over time, and for future generations, requires good management of the resources that provide the bedrock for people's well-being (including natural, human, economic, and social capital). The job of government is to manage these intergenerational resources well, and to promote people's well-being today, while also building what is needed to secure well-being for generations to come. And as good global citizens, societies increasingly need to consider whether actions taken in a national

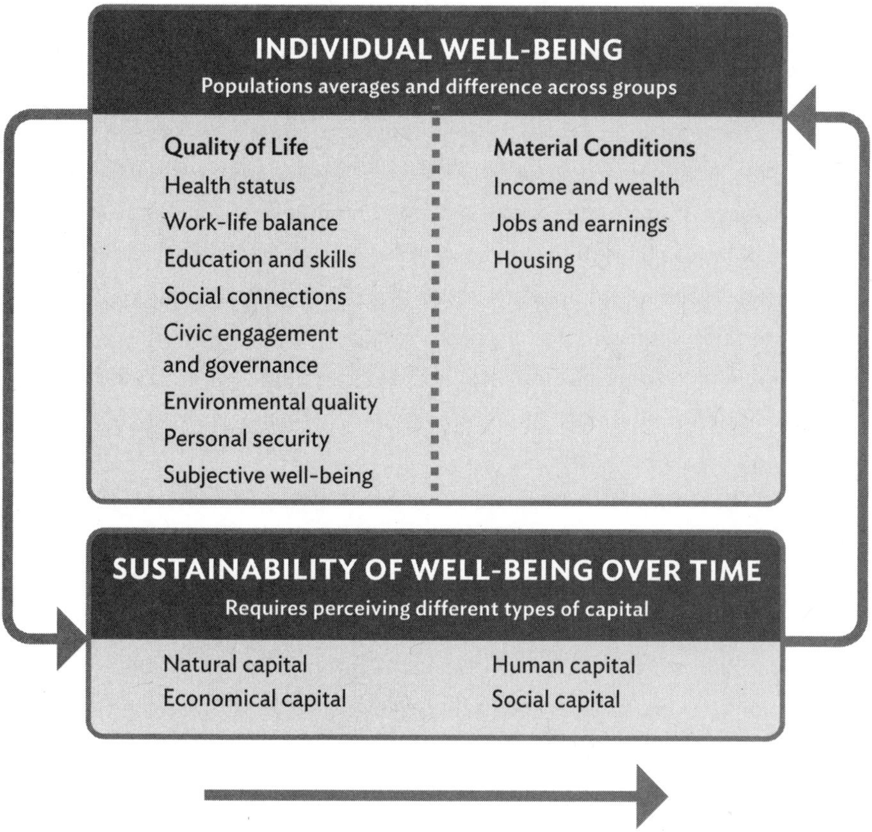

INDIVIDUAL WELL-BEING
Populations averages and difference across groups

Quality of Life	Material Conditions
Health status	Income and wealth
Work-life balance	Jobs and earnings
Education and skills	Housing
Social connections	
Civic engagement and governance	
Environmental quality	
Personal security	
Subjective well-being	

SUSTAINABILITY OF WELL-BEING OVER TIME
Requires perceiving different types of capital

Natural capital	Human capital
Economical capital	Social capital

FIGURE 6.1. The OECD's Well-Being Framework.
Credit: OECD *How's Life?* 2017.

context contribute positively or negatively to the global public goods (ranging from the atmosphere and oceans, to peace and security) on which all people depend for their well-being.

This means that to promote long-lasting happiness, government policies need to be assessed through three important lenses: first, for their impact on well-being *here and now*; second for their impact on well-being *later*; and third, for their impact on well-being *elsewhere*. In each of these cases, it is also important to think about distribution—i.e., will policy actions enhance the lives of many, rather than benefiting a few of those most well-off already, and are sufficient efforts being made to ensure that no one is left behind?

Better policies for better lives require good well-being data—but data alone are not enough to drive change. Although a range of economic, social, and environmental statistics are already available, they are most often used in ad hoc ways, and within policy silos, rather than as a holistic way to support decision making across all government departments. Often, decision makers lack the evidence, tools, and know-how to do this well. Sometimes, the economic imperative drives all other choices into the margins.

But times are changing. Several national governments are experimenting with practical policy tools and mechanisms to embed well-being more systematically in their decisions (see Exton and Shinwell, 2018; and Durand and Exton, 2019). These range from introducing well-being indicators in budget delibera-tions (for example, in France, Italy, New Zealand, and Sweden); drawing on well-being evidence to inform National Develop-ment Strategies and performance frameworks (in Slovenia, Scotland, and Paraguay); creating new institutional structures to champion well-being or support building the evidence base (e.g. in Ecuador, Wales, the United Arab Emirates, and the United Kingdom); and giving government analysts the support they need to consider well-being impacts in ex-ante appraisal and ex-post evaluation of specific policy proposals and pro-grams (e.g. New Zealand, the United Kingdom). Thoughtful and robust evaluation of these approaches, and the lessons learned, will provide a resource that can be shared internationally, and for future generations.

References

Durand, M. and C. Exton (2019). "Adopting a well-being approach in central government: Policy mechanisms and practical tools" *Global*

Happiness Policy Report 2019, Sustainable Development Solutions Network, New York.

Exton, C. and M. Shinwell (2018). "Policy use of well-being metrics: Describing countries' experiences", *OECD Statistics Working Papers*, No. 2018/07, OECD Publishing, Paris. doi.org/10.1787/d98eb8ed-en.

OECD (2017). *How's Life? 2017: Measuring Well-being*, OECD Publishing, Paris, doi.org/10.1787/how_life-2017-en

MARTINE DURAND is the OECD Chief Statistician, Director of the Statistics and Data Directorate. She is responsible for providing strategic orientation for the Organisation's statistical policy and oversees all of OECD's statistical activities. She is in particular responsible for the Organisation's work on the measurement of people's well-being and societal progress, promoting the analysis and use of well-being and sustainability indicators for policy-making. This work features regularly in the flagship publication *How's Life?* and related reports on well-being, inclusive growth, and sustainable development. She was formerly Deputy-Director of Employment, Labour and Social Affairs. Ms. Durand also worked for a number of years in the Economics Department. Ms. Durand graduated in mathematics, statistics, and economics from the Paris VI University, the Ecole Nationale de la Statistique et de l'Administration Economique (ENSAE), and the University of Wisconsin–Madison.

Example Proclamations

One person, such as a mayor, governor, minister, or president, can make a proclamation, or a group, such as a council or group of cabinet ministers. A model happiness proclamation is provided in Appendix D for adoption or adaptation. It can be changed and amended to fit the goals and circumstances of policymakers and community organizers.

The model proclamation has been used by heads of government as well as elected bodies. It was first used by the Seattle City Council in 2011, and then later used by officials ranging from the mayor of Cali, Colombia, (where it was translated into Spanish) and the city manager of Eau Claire, Wisconsin. It has also been adapted for use by heads of educational institutions and other agencies. In some cases, a press conference occurred upon its issuance, and in other cases an event such as a town hall meeting was held. In Kuwait, rather than issue a proclamation, a single statement announcing the government's intentions was posted on Twitter. In other instances, such as at several universities, the proclamation was issued to or by students, staff, and faculty rather than to the public at large.

The model proclamation is provided for adoption and adaptation. Some phrases will be useful without alteration, others will need to be altered, replaced, or cut, depending on the circumstances.

Working with the Media

Prior to the release of the proclamation, contact your local media to generate interest in the story. If possible, give the media advance notice of a press release. Governmental agencies and departments often have relationships with the media and can build on these to prepare and educate the media. City or regional governments may work with the media and other community representatives as part of the process of integrating happiness into public policy, thereby ensuring the media is educated and aware prior to issuing a press release.

A press release should accompany the release of a proclamation. Press releases generally follow a set format. The header includes the phrase *for immediate release*, all in caps, followed by the date. The second line gives the title of the release, and the third line gives contact information so the media can call for interviews. The body of the press release begins with the name of the town or city in all caps, followed by an introductory sentence, a need statement, project description, motivational statement, supporting statement, and call to action. A model press release is provided in Appendix E. It has been drafted to announce the measurement of happiness of a people, and can be adapted for any other purpose.

A press statement is released by sending it to local and national media and publishing it on the relevant website. Once the press release is published, it is important that the persons identified as media contacts are available, as reporters often work on short timelines.

Sometimes a reporter will have a negative reaction, stating that happiness is not the business of government. In such cases, it is important to remain focused on the purpose and intent of the effort. It is often best to clearly state that the purpose of government is to secure people's inalienable right to the pursuit of happiness (the US Declaration of Independence states the pursuit of happiness as an inalienable right of citizens), and to clarify the ways in which the government's effort is working to this end. Citing other governments, such as the United Kingdom, Bhutan, and United Arab Emirates, that are also focusing on happiness and well-being and educating the media and public about the definition of happiness can also be helpful when countering negative media. Community organizers and other stakeholders can also be asked to write op-eds and post comments to clarify and educate reporters.

The media may also express a fear that the government will enforce happiness behaviors upon people. In such cases, it is important to clarify that the purpose of the effort is to provide the opportunity for people to pursue their own happiness, as they define it for themselves. Examples of this can be given. One example is destigmatizing mental illness care and providing greater access to mental health care. Another example is opening channels for people to volunteer at community-based organizations or with governmental agencies such as parks departments. Such examples can be used to show that in neither case are people being forced to take action, but rather provided opportunities that are known to have beneficial impacts on most people's happiness and well-being.

7

Action Plan:
Happiness Roles and Responsibilities

It may not be enough to pass proclamations, measure happiness, or provide tools and resources for policymakers. Leadership is often needed to provide expertise, strategize, shepherd the process, and troubleshoot. This need can be filled by appointing a happiness official. A happiness official can be a high-level leader, such as a minister, or a set of high-level leaders, such as directors or officers for different levels, branches, or departments of government, or both. The high-level happiness officials may have staff, work with officers within departments or levels of government, or a combination of both. Within departments or levels of government, there is also a need for leadership. This need can be filled by appointing mid- or lower-level officials, such as coordinators or team leaders, who work with the higher level officials. When naming the official, it is important to use titles that do not attract unnecessary derision or suspicion. For example, the use of the term minister or director is preferable to supervisor or manager, where the term supervisor could lead people to feel that their emotional state is subject to being controlled.

Happiness officials are responsible for integrating happiness and well-being into an entity and its processes. They determine the means that happiness and well-being will become a focus for government, bring in the resources, and work with departments, administers, and elected officials. Happiness officials work with each aspect of government to facilitate the understanding and use of happiness as government's ultimate goal. This should be done with the understanding that the term happiness encompasses the concepts of thriving, well-being, quality of life, resilience, and sustainability. A comprehensive approach is necessary to make a significant and lasting difference, but it is important to take an approach that best suits the conditions and circumstances of an effort, so that people in government feel encouraged and enabled in the tasks ahead. Appendix F: Model Happiness Minister or Officer Job Description lists responsibilities that describe the tasks entailed to integrate happiness into office. This model description can be adopted or adapted in whole or part.

There are two approaches to creating the role of a happiness official in government: appointing or integrating. The integrating approach entails adding responsibilities to already existing positions and/or departments. The bureau of statistics for an area, a national or regional department, or the office of a mayor may choose to adopt happiness measurements and goals and form policies based on these measurements and goals or simply report on the happiness of the people. The integrating approach was taken by the national government of the United Kingdom, the Minister of National Development Planning for Indonesia, and the mayor of Bhopal in India. The approach of appointing entails creating a new position. The new position may be a Minister, Officer, or Coordinator of Happiness. The appointing approach was taken in Bhutan, the United Arab Emirates, and Santa Monica, California. It is important to note that for both approaches, the end goal should be to ensure that government places the happiness of its people as its highest priority.

Integrating Happiness Roles and Responsibilities

The government of Bhutan was the first to adopt happiness into its constitution, which states "(T)he State shall strive to promote those conditions that will enable the pursuit of Gross National Happiness" in the second clause of the ninth article.[1] Taking a similar approach to Bhutan but on a different matter, the nation

POLICY HIGHLIGHT
Dubai's Happiness Agenda and Happiness Champions

by Ali al-Azzawi

The happiest city on Earth—this is the vision that Dubai is following, as declared by His Highness Sheikh Mohammed Bin Rashid Al Maktoum (Vice President and Prime Minister of the UAE and Ruler of Dubai). The declaration was emphasized during his launch in May 2016 of Smart Dubai's Happiness Agenda, which is the tool to achieve this vision. The Happiness Agenda itself is composed of four portfolios of projects focused on delivering specific outcomes, underpinned by solid scientific foundations regarding the notion of happiness and well-being. The portfolios are: Discover, Educate, Change, and Measure. Briefly, the Discover portfolio aims to achieve a shared language and common understanding of people's needs in the city. The Educate portfolio is focused on increasing awareness around good practice and understanding of happiness and associated methods, and the Change portfolio is concerned with relevant interventions and policies. Finally, the Measure portfolio attends to the various ways of measuring happiness, in order to close the feedback loop, and ensure an efficient and efficacious process. Still, a city has a variety of domains that influence the happiness of its residents and visitors, such as trust, mobility, sociality, service quality, security and safety, urban design, and place-making (see the *Global Happiness Policy Report 2018*). However, one challenge facing city-wide organizations, such as Smart Dubai, is regarding how to orchestrate and coordinate happiness-related activities within the city, in an efficient way that is consistent with the premise of a smart city, minimizing effort and resources, while maximizing the desired outcome of social benefit and a happy city. A socially smart city.

Smart Dubai's answer to this challenge was to create the Happiness Champions network. This is comprised of senior staff in each government and nongovernment entities (representing the majority of domains in the city), who have access to the Director General, and executive operational roles and happiness-related activities within their organization. In turn, Smart Dubai has its own Happiness Champion, whose role is to coordinate and organize the network, using various activities. In this way, Smart Dubai is able to ensure consistent and efficient effort in the city, and enable knowledge sharing and collaboration within the network, where the champions consistently report on the positive value they gain from connecting and learning from each other, including the healthy competitive environment, to help them in their own work. This system ensures a decentralized locus of effort, while still maintaining a core center for knowledge sharing and organization. Each entity conducts their own activities, yet all have clear visibility of each other's activities, avoiding duplicate effort, and taking advantage of opportunities to multiply and scale their effort in the city.

Crucially, this is not just an interest group. With forty-seven champions across forty entities, the network has a mix of regular formal and informal meetings, with quick and efficient communication channels, in order to disseminate knowledge and experience across the city. The champions play an active role, such as taking part in various practical training activities, leading to tangible projects being deployed in the city. These training activities range from pre-prescribed courses such as service design, to bespoke programs that are conducted in the context of cities that perform well in global happiness rankings.

These programs usually lead to both collaborative and individual projects that apply their learnings. The regular gatherings also enhance experience sharing, such as success stories from applying analysis of the Happiness Meter data (collected at service points throughout the city), which helps other champions to see practical examples of how to enhance happiness in the city. In this way, the champions network actively breaks down any potentially isolated behavior, leading to a happier and more cohesive city.

ALI AL-AZZAWI is the City Experience Advisor responsible for the Happiness Agenda at Smart Dubai Office (SDO), focusing on the development of the scientific foundations and assessment methods that underpin its activities. His academic and professional interests center on the theory and applications of smart technologies towards city-wide policies and activities towards happiness and well-being. His academic and working experience started with physics, electronics, and computing, at the University of Oxford and Dartmouth College, later moving to the commercial sector, installing, developing, and supporting research MRI equipment around the world. With a strong interest in how people use technology and their customer experience, he undertook his PhD research at the Psychology Department and the Digital World Research Centre (University of Surrey, UK), where he has remained as a Visiting Research Fellow. He has a growing list of publications, including his book on the psychology of people's *Experience with Technology*, currently being used as a core text at some graduate courses. Most recently, he setup and led the first government-based CX Lab in the Middle East, where he also leads research and design, winning multiple-awards, including the complex omni-channel government service portal (DubaiNow), Dubai Smart City Platform (Dubai Pulse), and Dubai's Happiness Meter.

of Ecuador has recognized the rights of nature in its constitution. These include the right of restoration, of prevention of extinction of species and ecosystem destruction, and of people to benefit from nature for enjoyment purposes.[2]

The United Kingdom was among the first in the West to experiment with integrating happiness into a governmental department. In 2010, the Office of National Statistics (ONS) expanded its duties and now gathers subjective well-being data.[3] The ONS also brought together a comprehensive set of metrics for measuring well-being that included subjective and objective metrics for economic, environmental, and social conditions, called the *Measures of National Well-being*. Inside the government, the Behavioural Insights Team, popularly called the "nudge department," used happiness and well-being data to encourage behaviors such as volunteering and donating. Within a few years of its formation, the department became a company, partly owned by the government. In the United Kingdom, other departments also used the happiness and well-being data gathered by the ONS to inform various aspects of policy.[4]

The Indonesian Ministry of National Development Planning (also called BEPPNAS) took an integrating approach as well. BEPPNAS is also responsible for progress towards the United Nations Sustainable Development Goals (SDG). BEPPNAS added the gathering of happiness data for aspects of affect, flourishing, and satisfaction with life to its task of gathering data for the SDGs. It also formulated a theory of happiness to fit within the cultural context of the country and the overall goals of the SDGs, whereby economic growth is an outcome of the happiness of the people.[5]

Integrating happiness responsibilities into a governmental department or office can be a good approach when the following four factors are in place:

1. Leadership of the department has a vision for the integration and strongly supports the effort.

2. People who are responsible are knowledgeable and willing.
3. Adequate time and resources are allocated.
4. Those who take on the additional responsibilities are rewarded for successful fulfillment of their additional tasks.

In the United Kingdom, the ONS successfully incorporated measurements of happiness and well-being into their processes, but by and large, policymakers promulgating policy and providing programs are not sure how to use the data. Much effort has gone into explaining how to use it by nonprofits and thought leadership.[6] This kind of work can support integration efforts but cannot replace any of these four factors necessary for successful integration of happiness responsibilities.

Appointing Happiness Roles and Responsibilities

Bhutan was the first country to create a happiness office, entitled the Secretary of the Gross National Happiness Commission. The Secretary of the Gross National Happiness (GNH) Commission works with other officials to integrate happiness into all aspects of government.[7] A complete list of its tasks ranges from using the GNH index as a "guide" and "monitoring stick" to forming five-year plans, and from overseeing smooth functioning of government agencies to budgeting.

In the United Arab Emirates, Her Excellency Ohood bint Khalfan Al Roumi was appointed as Minister of State of Happiness in 2016. She is tasked with integrating happiness into government and business and well as investigating happiness metrics for wider use.[8]

In the state of Madhya Pradesh, India, the Chief Minister, Shivraj Singh Chouhan, inspired by Bhutan, created the office of Happiness Minister.[9] He also holds the office. Chouhan set plans to create a department of happiness that would include positions of president, chief officer, research director, coordinators, and assistants. A panel of experts was convened to advise the efforts.

The Happiness Minister's office and staff should sit within government in such a way that it can work with every department or function. In some cases, such as in Bhutan, the happiness office seat is primarily that of coordinator and facilitator for dissemination of information, knowledge, and cooperation between the various governmental functions. In other governments, such as in United Arab Emirates, the happiness office sits within a high level of government, such as the President or Prime Minister, Governor or Director. In the long run, it should not be a separate department, nor should it be an administrative agency. In all cases, the recommendation is that the happiness office's function is not to promulgate specific policies or manage programs as a separate branch of government, but to work towards the goal of integrating happiness across government departments.

As a function of the top executive level of government, the happiness ministry and its officials should work to integrate happiness into every aspect of government. This includes cooperating with various government offices in the functions of planning, policy and program promulgation and management, implementation and use of metrics to measure performance, policy screening tools, and overall governmental performance reporting.

Over time, the Happiness Minister or Officer should have a staff of people proficient and experienced in each department of government to work as emissaries between the happiness office and each governmental department to fully integrate happiness into the functioning of government or work with designated people within each department to pursue this goal. The designated happiness liaisons should work within each department to educate and train civil servants to fully integrate happiness into all aspects of government so that eventually the happiness office staff people's role is simply to coordinate and facilitate between or within a department and securing people's pursuit of happiness becomes a natural way of governing.

8

Action Plan:
Community Engagement

The onset of an effort in community engagement can serve two functions: gathering information and broadcasting it. It also helps set the foundation for involvement later in a process. Community engagement comes in many forms. In this section, broadcasting information through social media is covered, as well as gathering information through convening a council and by engaging the public at large through a variety of mechanisms.

Engaging Through Social Media

Social media sites are increasingly used by public policymakers, from presidents of nations and cabinet ministers to departmental staff. Twitter, Instagram, LinkedIn, YouTube, and Facebook are among the more popular social media sites they use.

Unskillful use of social media can result in great damage to a reputation or program. It is important that social media users have clear guidelines regarding content that is posted. It is also important that clear guidelines are set regarding social media profiles. Moreover, successfully engaging through social media can be time consuming. Depending on the situation, it may be wise to employ a social media manager to manage social media or work with people who are using social media. Also depending on the situation, legal counsel or the legal department can be helpful in drawing up guidelines for social media use. Although there are risks in using social media, it can be a powerful aid in successfully integrating happiness and well-being policies, programs, and projects into government.

When defining guidelines for social media, there are four factors to consider: 1) purpose, 2) content, 3) profile, and 4) audience. Appendix G: Social Media Guide presents approaches and tips for each of these factors.

Convening a Happiness Council

The function of a council, also called a panel of experts or advisors, is to provide advice, lend expertise, and help advance the goals of the government when appropriate. Convening a happiness council can also lend gravitas because of the people who are on the council. Experts on a council can also convey theory and intent by their membership in the council. Councils may be formed before a process is undertaken, to advise on strategy and other aspects of an endeavor, or at a certain point in a process to help advance a goal or initiative.

Global Councils

Global councils are largely composed of experts from outside the borders of a region. Global councils have been used to advise on specific activities, such as how to measure happiness and well-being, as was done by the city of Santa Monica, California.[1] They can also be convened for general guidance as was done by the United Arab Emirates.[2] Global councils can provide happiness movement expertise in the areas of research, measurements, and policies, as well as for specific fields, such as public-private sector enterprises, energy policies, or employee training programs. There are several well-known experts in the happiness movement who should be considered when convening a global council. These include the editors of the *World Happiness Report*, John Helliwell, Richard Layard, and Jeffrey Sachs. Enrico Giovannini, Jon Hall, and Martine Durant, authors of the OECD Better Life Index—a measurement that goes beyond GDP—are also world renowned happiness experts. Other world renowned experts in the happiness movement are Joseph Stiglitz, coauthor of the *Stiglitz-Sen-Fitoussi Report*, Gus O'Donnell of the Legatum Institute, and Andrew Clark of the Paris School of Economics.

A global council may also include subject area experts, such as experts in education, health, or workplace policy. Subject area experts can be found as contributing authors to chapters in the *World Happiness Report* or *Global Happiness Policy Report*. Subject area experts can also be identified through rosters for the European Commission's Beyond GDP—Measuring Progress, True Wealth and Well-being of Nations conference, the UAE's Global Dialogue for Happiness conferences, and some tracks of the OECD World Forums on Statistics Knowledge and Policy. A search for subject area experts using these sources will also yield other sources for identifying subject area experts.

There are also several well-known experts in the positive psychology movement who have been included on happiness councils. These include Martin Seligman, Mihaly Csikszentmihalyi, Sonja Lyubomirsky, Dan Buettner, and others. These are just a few global happiness movement experts and more can be identified through their co-authorship of books, articles, and reports.

Local Councils

Local councils are often composed of representatives of organizations that will be helpful in raising awareness and educating the public. They may provide resources such as time, staff, funding, and expertise, or implement aspects of a process or project, as was done in Victoria, British Columbia.[3] Local council members often include highly regarded members of a society who, when they speak about their contribution to an effort, will be listened to with respect. Members may also include subject area experts as well as members of underrepresented groups, such as youth, immigrant populations, or minorities.

Community Forums

Community forums provide ways to raise awareness, share information, garner support, and gather feedback. They are usually used as much to dispense information as to gather input from people. Community forums may be ongoing, such as with online portals, or singular events, such as town hall meetings.

POLICY HIGHLIGHT

Community Well-Being Asset Accounting in Alberta, Canada

by Mark Anielski

The word *wealth* comes from the thirteenth-century Old English *wela* meaning "the conditions of well-being." Happiness comes from the Greek *eudaemonia*, which Aristotle defined as "the well-being of spirit" (or soul). Hence, an economic assessment of the well-being of organizations or communities entails measuring how people perceive their well-being.

Measuring well-being in communities means measuring the physical and qualitative conditions of well-being of five key assets: human, social, natural, built, and financial/economic. In the town of Valleyview, Alberta (about 2,000 people), an engagement process that included representatives of the local government, nonprofits, schools, and business was undertaken. The town designed a well-being accounting and community asset governance system and conducted a comprehensive inventory of well-being using over a hundred objective measures of economic, social, health, and environmental well-being along with a comprehensive personal well-being survey of both children (aged eleven years and older) and adults.

As part of the inventory, people were asked to self-assess

their happiness, life satisfaction, spirituality, health, diet, relationship with family and neighbors, feelings of personal safety and inclusion, and their feelings about the state of the economy and environment. They were also asked to identify their unique skills or gifts that they would want to share with their neighbors. John McKnight and Peter Block, in their book, *The Abundant Community: Awakening the Power of Families and Neighborhoods* term these *abundant community assets*. Residents were also asked to rate or grade all municipal services and amenities so that town council and administration would have a greater sense of the value people derive from their local property taxes for municipal services.

The result was a comprehensive *State of Well-being Report* for the town that can be used by any number of stakeholders in the community including town council. Moreover, a "community asset" accounting and management system has been built that allows decision makers to determine the well-being return on investment of programs and services that impact well-being, as perceived by citizens.

This is an important step towards building functioning economies of well-being, no matter what the scale, from a small town to a nation. Measuring and managing the "genuine" wealth of the communities we live in is finally addressing Robert Kennedy's lament about GDP (gross domestic product)—that it *fails to measure the things that make life worthwhile.*

References

Town of Valleyview: The 2016 Well-being Portrait wowvalleyview.files
.wordpress.com/2018/08/valleyview-community-wellbeing-report
-04-29-2017.pdf

An Economy of Well-being: Valleyview State of Well-being Report 2017
economyofwellbeing.com/articles/governments/valleyview-state
-of-well-being-report-2017/

MARK ANIELSKI is an economist specializing in the measurement of well-being and happiness. He is the author of *The Economics of Happiness: Building Genuine Wealth* (2007) and a new book, *An Economy of Well-being: Common Sense Tools for Building Genuine Wealth and Happiness* (2018). He is also former Adjunct Professor of Corporate Social Responsibility and Social Entrepreneurship at the University of Alberta's School of Business (2003–2012) and was founding professor of Sustainable Economics at the Bainbridge Graduate Institute near Seattle (2002–2006). He has advised many communities, nations, and corporations on how to measure well-being including China, French Polynesia, Bhutan, The Netherlands, Austria, Canada, and the US. He currently serves on the Province of Alberta's Public Audit Committee which advises the government on issues related to accounting policies, financial statements, and audit reports. He lives in Edmonton, Alberta, Canada.

Online Portals

Websites, social media, and other digital means are often used to gather ideas and garner involvement. Often the question asked on an online portal is something about the nature of the project, program, or policy people would like to see implemented to enhance their happiness and well-being. In Dubai, an online portal modeled after a cultural tradition, called the Smart Majlis ("majlis" means a gathering, council, or assembly), was used to gather ideas from citizens and residents.[4] People were allowed to copyright their idea and if it was used by the government, they were compensated for it. Sometimes online portals are used to help people find volunteer opportunities as part of a program to increase happiness. People who want to volunteer are connected to local agencies or nonprofits who can give them opportunities such as planting trees, weeding in a park, tutoring, or helping at a food bank or shelter.

Online portals can also be used to gauge an idea of people's reaction to information. Social media sites, such as those mentioned above, as well as others such as WhatsApp, WeChat, and any number of other applications are used to gather reactions and feedback in real time.

Town Hall Meetings

Town hall meetings are speaking events in which information is presented by one or more speakers followed by a question and answer period. They have been used as part of a signing ceremony for a proclamation, and to build interest. A prominent researcher or author may be brought in to excite interest. A series of town hall meetings featuring different speakers for the domains of happiness (i.e., community, economics, education, environment, government, health, human settlements, psychology, social support, and time balance) can be part of an ongoing effort to raise awareness and gain engagement. Town hall meetings usually include a question and answer period and are sometimes recorded and put online.

Town hall meetings are open to the public. They are usually one- to two-hour events. A seminar or workshop may accompany a town hall style meeting. Conferences or forums can also be ways to educate and engage the public, government staff, and others. Sometimes it may be helpful to accompany town hall meetings with closed or invitation-only events for government staff and select constituents to educate and engage. In Dubai, the World Government Summit (an invitation-only event) includes the Global Dialogue on Happiness and many other closed working-group meetings and forums among national leaders, councils, and other smaller groups.[5]

World Café Style Meetings

World café style meetings are participatory events in which feedback from attendants is gathered in an informal and friendly way. This methodology for gathering feedback was developed by The World Café Community Foundation (see theworldcafe .com). World café style meetings have been used by governments, universities, and community organizations for projects ranging from national conferences and city-wide forums to small classrooms. They have been used in person with small and large groups and online.

People are invited with a stated purpose for the meeting, such as giving feedback on happiness data gathered for the area of the invitees. A presentation is given, such as an analysis of happiness data. Tables seating four or five people are set up with paper and writing instruments on them. Sometimes a large sheet of paper is taped to the table for people to write, draw, or sketch. Each table has a table captain who facilitates the process and takes notes. A specific topic is assigned to each table, such as a response to low or high scores for one question or domain, or a question is asked to the entire room and all tables focus on the answer to the question. People go from table to table giving their feedback and listening to each other in rounds or stay at a table as they see fit. At the end of the meeting, each table captain gives a short presentation synopsizing the feedback. A report is written capturing the feedback from each table. This process was used in various neighborhoods in the city of Itapetininga, São Paulo, Brazil, by the Instituto Visão Futuro in a series of projects.[6] It was also used in Victoria, British Columbia, for the first iteration of their happiness data gathering project.[7]

Besides social media, councils, and world café style meetings, there are many other ways to engage communities. When instituting happiness into public policy, using the channels already in place is wise. Adding new ones may provide opportunities to reach new audiences. With the use of various channels for community engagement, lessons will emerge. Over time, new media, particularly social media platforms, arise. Having a clear purpose for each community engagement method is helpful in choosing wisely the way to engage community.

POLICY HIGHLIGHT

Partnerships for Happiness

by John Helliwell

Successful happiness policies are characterized by buy-in from all levels of the organization (and often across ministries and disciplines), long-term commitments, continuity, flat structures, freedom to innovate, and fearless reporting of results, whether they are favorable or not. But existing bureaucratic structures, especially at the national level, are typically not able to deliver even a fraction of these characteristics. Yet there is growing interest among the public, and even within government policy circles, to redirect policies so as to enable happier lives.

Perhaps what is needed is to create safe spaces for happiness innovations that do not require ministries or whole national governments to go too far outside their comfort zones. One common element of successful examples is their ability to get collaboration and cooperation without excessive commitments—to achieve desirability while maintaining deniability. These examples might collectively be described as Partnerships for Happiness, each created for a specific purpose, usually on an initially small scale, and being quite explicitly experimental in nature. At the national level, the UK appears to have a bigger variety of such partnerships, including What Works Well-Being,[1] Happy City Bristol,[2] Action for Happiness,[3] the Behavioural Insights Team,[4] and many others. All of these organizations have secured cooperation from interested government departments, most importantly in the form of robust collection of happiness data and support for the underlying research, but including the provision of issues and expertise, and the reform of project evaluation to grant primacy to better lives as measured by peoples' own evaluations. Yet all of these activities and ventures are removed enough from the central engines of government so that their progress and results do not require a central policy commitment, and are at a sufficient distance that deniability is at hand for experiments that do not pan out, or that fail in ways that might be embarrassing to the government.

Partnerships for Happiness can operate as easily across ministries as within them, and are not restricted in the range of interventions or benefits to be considered, or how the costs and gains might be allocated across budget items. Most Partnerships for Happiness have not had their origins in government, but in the minds and with the leadership of those who see opportunities and simply try to assemble the elements required to produce happiness. They achieve their success by being small, nimble, and opportunistic in finding support where they can. In all cases the leaders tend to have had experience and connections within a particular interest or organization and start with a promising idea for improving happiness. There is also a need for organizations, such as the Happiness Research Institute[5] in Copenhagen, and the Happiness Alliance,[6] that can act as clearing houses for ideas for future partnerships for happiness. In many cities there are grant-making foundations that have the means and credibility to provide seed money and linkage opportunities for fledgling partnerships.

National governments can choose the degree of support they provide for Partnerships for Happiness. At a minimum, this support should include the appropriate redirection of national statistical efforts and establishing suitable methods for evaluating projects across government but could and should extend to collaboration and partial funding of agencies that are either themselves partnerships for happiness or can help to incubate new ones.

References

1. whatworkswellbeing.org
2. happycity.org.uk
3. actionforhappiness.org
4. behaviouralinsights.co.uk
5. happinessresearchinstitute.com
6. happycounts.org (Happiness Alliance)

JOHN F. HELLIWELL is co-editor and contributor of the *World Happiness Reports* and *Global Happiness Policy Reports*. He is an Arthur J. E. Child Foundation Fellow of the Canadian Institute for Advanced Research and co-director of CIFAR's program on "Social Interactions, Identity and Well-Being." He is also Professor Emeritus of Economics at the University of British Columbia, a member of the National Statistics Council, and a Research Associate of the National Bureau of Economic Research. He was visiting special advisor at the Bank of Canada in 2003–04, visiting research fellow of Merton College, Oxford, in 2003, of St. Catherine's College, Oxford, in 2001, and Mackenzie King Visiting Professor of Canadian Studies at Harvard 1991–94. He is a Fellow of the Royal Society of Canada and an Officer of the Order of Canada.

9

Action Plan:

Measuring Happiness

Happiness is defined and measured in three different ways; feelings, eudaimonia, and satisfaction with life and the conditions of life. Feelings are also called positive affect for feelings such as joy, happiness, calm, and contentment.[1] Negative affect is the term for feelings such as anger, hatred, sadness, and confusion. Eudaimonia is also called flourishing and includes feelings of being worthwhile, sense of purpose in life, optimism, level of engagement, and sense of accomplishment and of positivity.

These three aspects provide different information that can be used for various purposes. Data about affect can be used to understand how a specific environment or situation impacts people in the moment. For example, are people happier or more anxious working remotely or in the office; when commuting to work on the bus or in their car; or at a park or at home? Data on satisfaction with life and the conditions of life can be used to understand how people think about their experiences in life and whether people will want to move, change jobs, or make other life decisions.[2] For example, do people find their neighborhood or city to be safe or not, do they determine various jobs to be more or less satisfying, are they more or less happy with their relationship, or do they have an easier or harder time getting by between paychecks? Eudaimonia data can be used to understand whether people are fulfilling their potential and flourishing in their jobs, home life, and communities.[3]

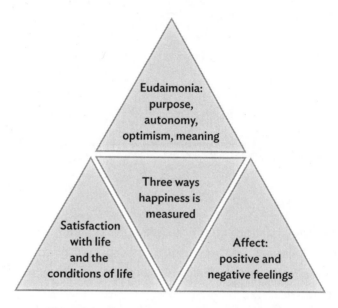

FIGURE 9.1. Three Ways Happiness Is Measured.

POLICY HIGHLIGHT

Well-Being Metrics in Policy

by Carol Graham

We live in the midst of progress paradoxes. Economic development has been unprecedented in the past decades, as evidenced by improvements in longevity, health, and literacy. Yet challenges remain, such as climate change, persistent poverty in some countries, and increasing income inequality, anomie, and unhappiness in many of the richest ones. In China, India, and the US, recent years have highlighted progress paradoxes where positive economic indicators coincide with rising rates of suicide and other premature deaths.

Well-being metrics, which capture the income *and* non-income determinants of reported human well-being, provide a different picture—beyond GDP—of what is happening to individuals within and across countries. They serve as important complements to traditional income-based data and provide insights into policies that can sustain human welfare in the future.

Scholars have developed robust knowledge about the determinants of well-being across individuals, countries, and time, with the standard variables showing remarkably consistent patterns. More recently, research links higher levels of individual well-being to better future outcomes.

The metrics are good for informing questions to which standard revealed preferences approaches—based on observed consumption choices—do not provide answers. These include the welfare effects of institutional arrangements individuals cannot change, such as inequality and pollution, and the explanation of behaviors driven by norms, addiction, or self-control problems.

The metrics provide insights into how humans experience and assess economic processes. They help explain adaptive preferences due to low expectations, preferences for equity, the role of stigma, and more. The metrics show that sufficient income is necessary to well-being. Yet they also highlight factors that are as, if not more, important, ranging from good health to meaningful work to fairness and friendships, and allow us to assess the relative weights that individuals place on them.

There is now established best practice on the need to measure *three distinct dimensions of well-being*: hedonic, evaluative, and eudaimonic. Each reveal different elements of human lives, from daily moods to life course evaluations to purposefulness.

The surveys do not ask respondents if particular things (such as income) or activities (such as commuting) make them happy, rather well-being questions are up front in the surveys. Scholars then analyze the data via econometric equations that control for standard socioeconomic and demographic traits, while unobservable innate traits are in the error term. Controlling for these variables, we can explore the well-being associations of those that vary, such as smoking or exercising, and institutional arrangements such as inequality and governance. Methodological challenges remain—as in all data collection—and involve constant innovation. Recent work shows how vignettes accompanying specific survey questions can address the challenges of adaptation and different scale norms, for example.

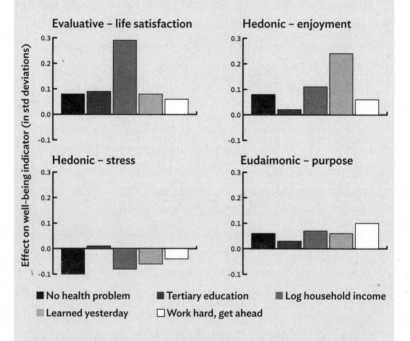

Figure 9.2. How Income Does (and Does Not) Matter to Three Well-Being Dimensions. Source: Author calculations based on Gallup World Poll 2009–2017. Bars obtained from regressing respective well-being indicators on socioeconomic and demographic controls (all binary, except household income)—with time and country fixed effects. Variables standardized: bars represent the change in the well-being indicator associated with a 1 standard deviation change in the corresponding variable.

Governments around the world, including the UK, Canada, and Chile, have begun to include the metrics in their regular statistics to help design and assess a range of policies. The OECD has published established best measurement practices, so that the results are comparable across countries and time, as are GDP indicators.

Debates continue about the extent to which well-being should be an *input* into policy evaluation or an *objective* of policy. In our view, the disaggregated data provide the most robust inputs, while the aggregate indicators can serve as warning lights—that highlight vulnerabilities or positive trends that provide broader lessons—on a broader dashboard that includes GDP.

CAROL GRAHAM is Leo Pasvolsky Senior Fellow at the Brookings Institution, a College Park Professor at the University of Maryland, and a Senior Scientist at Gallup. She served on a National Academy of Sciences panel on well-being metrics for policy in 2012–13, a Pioneer Award from the Robert Wood Johnson Foundation in 2017, and a Lifetime Distinguished Scholar award from the International Society of Quality of Life Studies in 2018. From 2002–2004, she served as a Vice President at Brookings. She has also served as Special Advisor to the Vice President of the Inter-American Development Bank, as a Visiting Fellow in the Office of the Chief Economist of the World Bank, and as a consultant to the International Monetary Fund and the Harvard Institute for International Development. She is the author of numerous books and articles. Her most recent books are: *Happiness for All? Unequal Lives and Hopes in the Land of the Dream* (Princeton, 2012); *The Pursuit of Happiness: Toward an Economy of Well-Being* (Brookings, 2011); and *Happiness around the World: The Paradox of Happy Peasants and Miserable Millionaires* (Oxford University Press, 2010). This article draws from C. Graham, K. Laffan, and S. Pinto. "Well-Being in Metrics and Policy," *Science*, Vol. 362 (6412), October 19, 2018.

The question of whether happiness can be measured has been answered. The issuance of the *World Happiness Report* first in 2012, and then again in 2013, 2015, and annually thereafter, proves not just that happiness can be measured, but also shows how to measure it. Further clarifying this issue is the Organization for Economic Co-operation (OECD)'s *Guidelines on Measuring Subjective Well-being*. Thus, the question is not whether happiness *can* be measured (yes, it can), but rather, *what* to measure?

Subjective and Objective Indicators

Surveys gather subjective data, which reflects people's self-assessment of their lives and their life conditions. Objective data reflects facts, which can be measured through observation, such as income levels, rates of illness, and enrolment in schools. Together, subjective and objective data reveal a balanced picture when data for an objective indicator is analyzed alongside data for a subjective indicator, when the two indicators have relevance to each other. The following figure provides a list of both these types of indicators.

For example, subjective data gathered about sense of safety and objective data gathered about crime rates can give policymak-

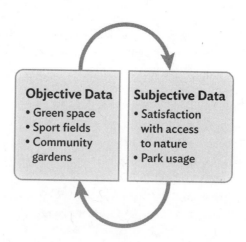

FIGURE 9.3. Examples of Subjective and Objective Indicators.

ers good information about the types and sorts of interventions needed. If subjective data reveals that people are unsatisfied with their access to nature and objective data reveals a growing number of plant and animal species are threatened or endangered, and there is a decline in open or green space in an area, policymakers and planners may consider ordinances and other means to encourage open and green spaces in the urban environments. The combination of subjective and objective data could instigate a study to understand how people in non-wealthy areas are meeting their needs. Findings could result in policy ideas to help populations in these areas where data based on surveys (self-evaluation or subjective data) gives decision makers new information and insights.

Governments of nations, regions, cities, or towns, have many sources of objective data that can be used to complement subjective data, from an agricultural department or census bureau to social security or veterans' administrations. In most cases, overabundance of available data rather than a dearth is the problem. Where there are gaps in data, nongovernmental organizations can be sources, from the World Bank to local issue-focused nonprofits.

One approach to collecting objective data to complement subjective data is to first align the domains or life circumstances for which there are both subjective and objective indicators. In the domains of the economy and standard of living, education, the environment, employment and work, health, government, social support, and human settlement, there are often data sets that paint a balanced picture. In some domains, such as aspects of community and psychological well-being, connecting subjective and objective data can be more challenging or require some assumptions and flexibility in using the data. For example, subjective data about optimism may be complemented with objective data about employment rates or labor market insecurity. Similarly, subjective data for feeling lonely could be complemented with objective data for mental illness rates, access to social services, or usage rates of family support programs.

How to Use Happiness Data in Brief

Happiness data reveals information about how people perceive themselves to be thriving or hurting. It is helpful in assessing the status of people's well-being and happiness in terms of ecological health, social support, income equality, meaningful employment, and many other conditions of life. Many of these life conditions are not considered when using gross domestic product (GDP) or other economic metrics, such as economic growth, consumption rates, or average income.

This data can be used to assess the impact of changes in policies or world events, and to evaluate the impact of an intervention. Such data can help point the way for promulgating policy that secures equal opportunities for all people's happiness. Happiness and well-being data also reveal enlightening information about varying dimensions of demographics, such as geographic information, age, gender, income levels, family size, and marital status, that objective data do not uncover.

Happiness data can be used as a guide for budgeting. When policymakers have to make difficult decisions about where to allocate resources or which programs to cut, happiness data can reveal where people are hurting the most, and which programs are more highly correlated to happiness and well-being. The Seattle City Council used happiness data in 2011, when lagging effects of the 2008 economic crisis impacted their budget, to decide not to close community centers due to low scores in a sense of community and high correlations between happiness and community.[4]

Happiness data can also be used for participatory budgeting, a process that allows the community to determine public budgeting decisions. In New York City, an online platform for participatory budgeting was used to gather ideas from citizens for eight years.[5] In the United Kingdom, participatory budgeting is more often used by neighborhood (borough) councils for small-scale projects in cities.[6]

The participatory budget process often involves brainstorming new ideas, creating project proposals, voting, funding, monitoring, and reporting. Happiness data can be incorporated into a participatory budgeting process to identify the needs of the community in conjunction with the input of the individuals and parties that participate in the process.

POLICY HIGHLIGHT

Well-Being Data Past, Present, and Future

by Ed Diener

I proposed in 2000 that we collect well-being data at the national level to serve as input for policy deliberations. The idea was to supplement economic data with variables such as life satisfaction and psychosocial flourishing to provide measures that broadly reflect well-being. Societal factors such as air pollution, commuting, and green spaces might not be reflected in the economic indicators, but are likely to be captured in people's reports of well-being, for example. Thus, well-being accounts provide valuable information in policy debates. In addition, leaders can profit from having information on what groups in society are flourishing versus floundering, and these individuals do not map perfectly onto income groupings.

More recently new findings have made the idea of national accounts of well-being even more compelling—based on the discovery that psychosocial well-being has very beneficial downstream benefits (e.g., Lyubomirsky et al., 2005; De Neve et al., 2013). It has been found that not only might health influence well-being, for example, but that well-being has an influence on health and longevity (Diener and Chan, 2011; Diener et al., 2017). Similarly, high psychosocial well-being seems to benefit supportive social relationships, good citizenship behavior, and altruism (Moore et al., 2018). At work, happy individuals and happy organizations seem to prosper more, with higher levels of performance (De Neve et al., 2019; Tenney et al., 2016). Many leaders who might not be overly concerned with "happiness" as a target for policy, will highly value factors that arise from well-being, such as better health, more supportive social relationships and citizenship, and higher work productivity. Thus, leaders often find the outcomes of happiness to be a more compelling reason to measure and raise it than simply trying to make people feel better.

The advances since 2000 in this area are notable. For instance, the United Kingdom adopted measures of well-being, and these allowed the increased funding of mental health services because the data showed that those suffering from mental illness have high levels of suffering. Organizations such as the Organisation of Economic Co-operation and Development have written on the use of well-being accounts for policy, and the United Nations adopted a resolution that well-being should be one goal of governments. We can expect to see even more use of well-being measures for policy in the decades ahead (see also Diener et al., 2015).

References

DeNeve, J-E., Diener, E., Tay, L., & Xuereb, C. (2013). The objective benefits of subjective well-being. In J. F. Helliwell, R. Layard, & J. Sachs (Eds.), *World happiness report 2013.* Volume 2. (pp. 54–79). New York: UN Sustainable Development Solutions Network.

Diener, E. (2000). Subjective well-being: The science of happiness, and a proposal for a national index. *American Psychologist,* 55, 34–43.

Diener, E., and Chan, M. Y. (2011). "Happy people live longer: Subjective well-being contributes to health and longevity." *Applied Psychology: Health and Well-Being,* 3, 1–43.

Diener, E., Oishi, S., and Lucas, R. E. (2015). "National accounts of subjective well-being." *American Psychologist,* 70, 234–242.

Diener, E., Pressman, S., Hunter, J., and Delgadillo-Chase, D. (2017). "If, why, and when subjective well-being influences health, and future needed research." *Applied Psychology: Health and Well-Being*, 9 (2), 133–167.

Lyubomirsky, S., King, L., and Diener, E. (2005). "The benefits of frequent positive affect: Does happiness lead to success?" *Psychological Bulletin*, 131, 803–855.

Moore, S., Diener, E., and Tan, L. (2018). "Happiness enhances social relationships." In Diener, E., Oishi, S., and Tay, L. (Editors). *Handbook of Subjective Well-Being*.

Tenney, E. R., Poole, J. M., and Diener, E. (2016). "Does positivity enhance work performance?: Why, when, and what we don't know." *Research in Organizational Behavior*, 36, 27–46.

ED DIENER is a Professor of Psychology at the University of Virginia, the University of Utah, and Senior Scientist for the Gallup Organization. He is one of the most eminent research psychologists in the world. With over 380 publications and a citation count over 180,000, he is one of the most highly-cited scholars in the world. He is widely considered the pioneer in well-being research. He has been a leader in the movement to use well-being metrics to help guide public policy. In his recent research Diener found that people high in well-being tend to be healthier and live longer, are more productive at work, are better citizens, are more creative, are more resilient, and have stronger and more stable social relationships. Following this lead, he has developed an intervention to raise well-being in adult populations, as well as developing it for specific groups such as counseling clients, employee assistance programs, and medical and nursing students.

How Happiness Is Measured Using Surveys

People's level of happiness and well-being can be measured by surveys.[7] To measure how someone is feeling or what they think about something, you simply ask. When asking about feelings, it is important to ask about one feeling at a time.[8] Ed Diener was one of the first to develop a survey to measure feelings. His affect scale includes twelve feelings: positive, negative, good, bad, pleasant, unpleasant, happy, sad, afraid, joyful, angry, and contented. It is up to each person to define how happiness, sadness, joy, anger, anxiety, calm, etc., feels to them. One person's sense of being happy may be very different from another person's, but both definitions are embedded in the term *happiness*.

To measure eudaimonia, one commonly uses what is called a *flourishing scale*. The flourishing scale asks questions about areas of optimism, positivity, purpose, engagement, accomplishment, and worthiness.

To measure satisfaction with life, one can use the Cantril Ladder question, asking whether their life is the best or worst possible life, as well as the question, "Overall, how satisfied are you with your life nowadays?" These two questions together in a survey represent the best practice to date.

To measure satisfaction with life's circumstances it is necessary to identify those circumstances. In the nation of Bhutan, where Gross National Happiness is measured using a survey instrument, the domains measured are: government, economy (standard of living), environment, culture, community, health, education, and time balance in addition to measures for satisfaction with life, affect, and eudaimonia. The OECD Better Life Index measures the domains of housing, income, jobs, community, education, environment, civic engagement, health, safety, work-life balance as well as measures for life satisfaction. In the United Kingdom, the Office of National Statistics (ONS) well-being survey (formerly called happiness survey) gathers psychological well-being data with four questions about happiness, anxiety, sense of worthiness, and satisfaction with life, and their measures of national well-being cover the domains of economy and personal finance, education and skills, employment, environment, government, health, housing, and relationships.

The Happiness Alliance's Happiness Index includes the Cantril Ladder as well as the four questions for psychological well-being within the UK ONS well-being survey. It also includes a flourishing scale based on questions from the OECD *Guidelines on Measuring Subjective Well-being* and work by Huppert and So as well as questions for the same domains as Bhutan's Gross National Happiness Index.

POLICY HIGHLIGHT

The Politics of Statistics

by Jon Hall

Official statisticians—those who work for national statistical offices (NSOs) around the world—rightly take pride in their impartiality and objectivity. The world of the NSO is one that focuses on data not politics. The mission statement of the Australian Bureau of Statistics, my former home, puts it well: "We assist and encourage informed decision-making, research and discussion within governments and the community, by providing a high quality, objective and responsive national statistical service." (Australian Bureau of Statistics, 2018)

In other words, statistics provide important support to the policy-making process, but the work of a statistician is apolitical. Or is it?

Every government statistician is taught—at a young age—that "you can't manage what you don't measure," to help justify the importance of official statistics. True enough. But what if the very act of measuring something causes it to become a priority for government action? Imagine if the numbers an NSO decides to collect inexorably shape a nation's direction. What could be more political than that? Yet this is exactly what happens, at least according to Joe Stiglitz who noted in 2009—when he and his colleagues released their seminal report on measuring economic performance and social progress—that once a nation starts measuring something it starts managing it because "what we measure affects what we do. If we have the wrong metrics, we will strive for the wrong things." (Stiglitz, 2009).

If you accept that argument, then it follows that the role of an NSO is intensely political. This is not a problem in itself, but it must, I believe, be explicitly recognized by statisticians and the broader community.

There is, however, a difference between work that is political and political work. If statisticians recognize how political their work can be, they should also recognize how important it is for them to strive to remain above politics. In every country someone, or some organization, must decide what data to collect. Who better to take that decision than an NSO, an organization that ought to be trusted to take decisions with as much objectivity as possible? The NSO's decisions will—almost always—be influenced by the political forces of the day. That is natural. It is the statisticians' job to be transparent about the role of that influence in their decision making and to be utterly apolitical in how the data are presented and analyzed.

The views expressed in this "Policy Highlight" are the author's and do not represent views of the United Nations Development Programme, the Human Development Report Office, nor of any other organization, agency, or program of the United Nations.

References
Australian Bureau of Statistics. (2018). https://bit.ly/2uSQRis

Jon Hall is a Policy Specialist for the United Nations Development Program. Jon has been thinking about how to quantify—and influence—national development since 2000. His 2002 work for the Australian Bureau of Statistics on Measuring Australia's Progress won a national award as the "smartest" social project of the year. From 2005—2009 he led the Global Project on Measuring the Progress of Societies at the OECD promoting these ideas around the world. Since 2012 has been working on strengthening national human development reporting. Jon has a masters degree in applied statistics and econometrics, and another in public service administration. He has lectured in over fifty countries and has a particular interest in measuring happiness. In 2013 he was one of ten "global opinion leaders" to meet with German Chancellor Angela Merkel to discuss his work. Jon is one of the contributors to the *World Happiness Reports*.

How to Measure Happiness

There are three questions to answer when measuring happiness. The first question is, "What measurements will be used?" The second question is, "How will the data be gathered?" The third question is, "Who will gather the data?"

Addressing the question of what measurements to use, it is crucial that the measurements used are validated. Validated measurements, ensure that the data collected actually reflects the happiness and well-being of those measured. Many different validated surveys are available for use, including the Happiness Alliance's Happiness Index, for which you can find the methodology and source of each question. Other surveys include the General Social Survey, the European Social Survey, the World Values Survey, the OECD Better Life Index (which includes objective metrics and survey data), and the Gallup World Poll. Happiness surveys should include questions about satisfaction with life, affect, and flourishing, as well as the circumstances or domains of life. Common domains across most happiness and well-being surveys are community and social support, culture, education and lifelong learning, environment, health, government, standard of living and the economy, time balance, and work. In some places a happiness officer, department, or other capacity develops questions specific to an area's circumstances. In this case, it is important to test that the questions reflect the intent of the query. In some cases, a government will add questions to surveys that are already in use. In other cases, governments will devise their own versions of questions or their own unique questions. Two important reasons for using survey questions that are already in use are that the questions are validated and data has been gathered for them which can be useful for comparisons.

The second question is, "How to gather data?" There are two ways to gather data: through a random sampling or a convenience sampling. In either case, it is important that data gathered is representative of the population. A random sampling ensures a representative sampling. Fewer people need to be surveyed for a random sampling, but the people who take the survey truly have to be selected randomly. There are many ways to calculate the appropriate size for a random sample. See any manner of statistical guides for this; we also provide an example in the endnotes.[9] More and more, cities and governments are using convenience sampling. Convenience sampling is economical and allows anyone the opportunity to take the survey. Data from convenience sampling is representative when a sufficient portion of the population participates in a survey, with the number of people who should be surveyed dependent upon the size of the population and based on the desired confidence level and margin of error. A higher confidence level or lower margin of error requires a larger sample size. Another way to test whether a convenience sampling is representative is to groundtruth it with data collected by a random sampling. This latter approach is gaining popularity among local governments. This approach entails a great deal of community outreach and media coverage to be successful.

Some governments, such as the mayor's offices of Victoria, British Columbia, Santa Monica, California, and Seattle, Washington, conduct a convenience sampling rather than a random sampling. Their success in gathering reliable data is in part due to robust media campaigns and support from the media and public. This strategy entails harnessing the resources of a community and has a double benefit of engaging organizations and people in the effort.

The third question is, "Who will gather the data?" Some governments include data gathering as one of the functions of a branch or office of government, particularly when that office is appointed. Governments that are already gathering data through surveys will often include the gathering of happiness data by the same agency or department that is already conducting surveys such as a statistics office or planning department. Some governments hire a consultancy. This can be the least economical way to go, but when a government needs representative data, has the budget, and does not have the capacity, this approach fits.

A model press release for announcing the gathering of data is provided in Appendix E. It is written for adaptation to an area, with sample quotes from past use. When governments conduct convenience samplings, representatives of the media are often engaged in the planning stage for gathering data. In such cases, media representatives may even help to circulate a press release to other media. Lastly, regarding press releases, it is important that the person or people who are listed as contact in the contact information are ready and available to the media once the press release is issued.

When gathering data with a survey, several questions are likely to arise. These include whether people can trust that their data will be secure and not misused, why they should take the survey, and what they gain from taking the survey. Appendix H: Questions and Answers for Happiness Survey Takers provides information that can be used and adapted to answer these questions.

The Happiness Index

The Happiness Alliance's Happiness Index is a scientifically valid measure of happiness and well-being. The text of the survey and an online platform for surveying a population can be found online at happycounts.org. The survey methodology has undergone peer review.[10]

Reflections on the Dynamics of Happiness

by Dennis Meadows

Efforts to quantify and measure happiness are extremely important. They can help reduce the fabulous preoccupation with GDP as an indicator of well-being; they will orient us towards more sustainable policies; and they may encourage people to start identifying what is really important to them. Happiness reports reflect people's interactions with complex social, economic, and physical systems. Happiness measures will be more useful when they better reflect one important behavior of those systems: "Better Before Worse."

Actions that make systems seem better in the short term often sow the seeds of longer-term consequences that eventually make the system seem worse. This predicament is seen at all levels. For example, using more fossil energy to ease the rigors of life now, will cause greater destruction of the climate later. You may choose work over study now to raise your short-term income, but that means reduced income options in the future. Using a credit card now to raise consumption will mean that future consumption is lower than it could have been, once the bills come due. Taking another alcoholic drink typically makes you happier now, but at the expense of a bigger headache tomorrow.

I easily could cite many hundreds more examples. Most of us manage to avoid these traps, because we can foresee the future costs of current actions. If we conclude those costs will outweigh the short-term gain, we avoid the temptation of an immediate, transient pleasure. But when the costs occur far in the future, they may be invisible or ignored. Then we can become enmeshed in the "Better Before Worse" trap.

Imagine you have a magic button. Press it now, and you will be completely happy for the rest of your life. But you will be killed tomorrow by a meteorite strike. I expect you would not press the button. Now assume that the strike will come twenty years in the future. The button is much more tempting. We need to design happiness surveys, so that those who have pressed that Faustian button do not automatically appear at the top of the list.

There are two paths to happiness—get what you want, or want what you get. We live within systems that habitually turn to the first option. And because our leaders typically have very short-term perspectives, they ignore the woes they are storing up for us by giving us more now.

The science of measuring happiness will be more useful when it does not do that.

DENNIS L. MEADOWS is Emeritus Professor of Systems Management at the University of New Hampshire. He has been the Director of three university research institutes: at MIT, Dartmouth College, and the University of New Hampshire. He received four honorary doctorates from universities in the US and Europe for his contributions to environment and education. He has co-authored ten books, including the 1972 report, *The Limits to Growth*. In 2018 he was inducted into the Earth Hall of Fame, Kyoto, Japan.

The Happiness Index is available for anyone to use. Survey takers receive their own self-assessment of their happiness alongside a comparison to others who have taken the survey. This presentation of data has been found to inform people about the definition of happiness and help people take meaningful action in their own lives.

Countries, states, counties, and cities have been using the Happiness Index since 2011. In that year, the cities of Seattle, Washington, and Eau Claire, Wisconsin, as well as the state of Vermont used it for budgeting, program, and other policy decisions. Since then, governments including Kuwait, the United Arab Emirates, and Creston District in Canada, Nevada City in the US, and others have used it.

It can be used via the online platform at happycounts.org or with permission from the Happiness Alliance (email info@happy counts.org). The full data set, except personal contact information, is also available for research purposes with personal data privacy and protection agreement. See Appendix I: The Happiness Index Questions for the questions in the Happiness Index.

POLICY HIGHLIGHT

Community Driven Happiness Data Collection

by Michael Moser

In 2013 the Center for Rural Studies (CRS), a nonprofit fee-for-service research center located at the University of Vermont's Department of Community Development and Applied Economics partnered with Gross National Happiness USA (GNHUSA) to develop and implement a happiness study that would be representative of Vermont's population. As the home of the Vermont State Data Center, a Census Bureau data liaison program, and as an organization concerned with collecting and supporting indicator data for Vermont communities, the Center for Rural Studies found the project to be a close fit with its mission. CRS would serve GNHUSA's goal of advancing happiness in the public discourse by providing a sound methodological approach to collecting data representative of the state population, while insights gained from this research would complement and enhance the Center's existing data sets and knowledge of Vermont communities.

The collaboration included the Happiness Alliance, using their Happiness Index as the basis for the survey instrument, and their national happiness database to make comparisons between national happiness levels and Vermonters' happiness levels. This collaboration enabled the development and implementation of a first-of-its-kind, Happiness & Well-being assessment that was statistically representative of a state's population.

The ability to attribute the results to the Vermont population overall and the ability to compare Vermonters' happiness levels to national happiness levels were factors that contributed to the implementation of a second round of Vermont happiness data collection that took place in 2017. This happiness collaboration has led to Vermont being the only US state with a longitudinal happiness dataset that is statistically representative of its population.

The *Vermont Happiness Reports* can be found on the University of Vermont's webpage Resources and Expertise to Support People and Communities at uvm.edu/crs/?Page=reports/report.html.

MICHAEL MOSER is a research specialist with the University of Vermont's Center for Rural Studies and also coordinates the Vermont State Data Center—a Census Bureau liaison program for Vermont. He has over a decade of experience designing and implementing research projects, working with population indicators and conducting outreach and education on where and how to access data that provides knowledge about population well-being. He experiences a high level of well-being living and working in his home state of Vermont.

Action Plan:
A Tool for Policy:
The Happiness Policy Screening Tool

The Happiness Policy Screening Tool allows policymakers a way to assess the happiness and well-being impact of a policy. It can also be used for programs and projects. It can be used in the early stages of promulgating a policy, forming a program, or creating a project to guide their formation, or to evaluate the benefits of a policy, program, or project under consideration for adoption or implementation. The Happiness Policy Screening Tool can be found in Appendix J.

POLICY HIGHLIGHT

From Origin to Application: Bhutan's GNH Index

*Excerpted from distinguished lecture at
the Sheldonian Theatre, University of Oxford*

Karma Ura

Happiness as the goal of governments and leadership occurs in various older textual sources in the Buddhist Himalayas. It is not surprising because Buddha's teaching is about happiness as the basic preference of sentient beings though "dukkha and samsara" are a natural order of things if allowed to happen, individually and collectively. Bhutan was founded by a Buddhist monk in 1626. His ultimate theoretical justification for forging a new nation was to have a country teeming with those who realized non-dual nature, where happiness and unhappiness would have no real duality, no real existence, not real fixed essential of anything.

Public policies now require measurable evidence and hence GNH index came. Originally, the aims behind GNH index were to (1) guide plans by benchmarking to indicators, (2) frame allocation of budget, (3) track changes of GNH over time, (4) compare Bhutan's performance with other nations by producing certain comparable statistics on life satisfaction, five life-domain satisfactions, and other elements. Bhutan designed a questionnaire by indigenizing content of questions as well as drawing much from western survey methods on wellbeing, happiness and quality of life. We then ran the survey foisting multi-item question on people most of whom were knowledgeable but illiterate peasants. In the early surveys face to face interview lasted four hours per respondent. Revision based on trial and error could reduce the interview time to two hours plus. The enumerators trekked across highly scattered settlements and visited the randomly pre-selected households included in the listing. Overall each field survey done every four years took six months to complete. A sample of 8,000 people 15 years or older is necessary for our results to be valid at the district level, in addition to being valid nationally.

GNH survey collects and computes numerous non-monetary variables except for a handful of monetary variables like income and assets linked to income. The GNH survey questionnaire consists of 135 questions, excluding 18 demographic questions. If we count in the most detailed way, 277 variables are actually used in the construction of 33 indicators and GNH single number composite index. The number of variables in the

GNH index depends on how they are counted. For example, if five life-domain satisfactions are aggregated and that sum is reported, it counts as one variable. Similarly, if the 12 General Health Questions scores are added and the subtotal is counted, it counts as one variable. By this method of counting, GNH index uses 130 variables. However, 277 is count of variables disaggregated to the level of each individual variable. Incidentally, if an individual were to achieve a perfect score in GNH index, it would have 277 achievements out of 277 variables.

Another feature of the GNH index is that it can be decomposed at any subsidiary level of domains and demography. Thus, GNH is a tool for analyzing distribution of happiness across the population as well as distribution of achievements that contribute and constitute happiness of an individual.

The concept of threshold applied to each individual's achievement with respect to each variable is central to GNH indicators. As an individual passes a threshold, indicating achievement in that variable, he or she obtains that condition contributing to happiness. The idea of threshold is closely related to the idea of sustainable and well distributed happiness. It may come as a surprise and an irony that in GNH index, if an individual passes certain number of thresholds, he or she is deemed to have the causes and conditions for happiness and excluded from any further part in the index. GNH index is focused on guiding policies to support individuals who experience under-achievement in terms of failing to pass a threshold. By excluding those who have passed the threshold from further calculation, the method explicitly tells the policymakers that policy intervention is, relatively, not a priority in the cases of those happy individuals as they already have it—the rest lies to some degree in the hands of policymakers. Policy focus encouraged by the GNH index is on those who have failed to achieve threshold level with respect to certain variables, so it is geared towards equity.

But I would like to stress that maximization of the scalar number GNH index by policy making is not possible by the government. No government can dictate, especially with respect to variables which are beyond the reach of state and are far more matters of habits, interpersonal relationships, beliefs and practices, which are part of their rights. Yet a government, as the ultimate reflection of individual citizens' aspirations and preferences, or of animals, for happiness, can always improve its tentative understanding of such personal, behavioral and relational facts where public policies can affect them. In addition, there are a large array of variables which are subject of direct public policy intervention.

There are five technically specific ways in which GNH indicators are being applied in the administration of the country at present. Firstly, GNH index and some of the domain indicators and sub-indicators are directly used as a bench mark in the Five Year Plan (FYP) to aim for further progress. At the overall national level, the FYP is guided by national targets and key results. In the current plan, 17 baselines or targets are drawn from GNH indicators such as sufficiency level in mental health, safety, community vitality, skills, political participation, fundamental rights, SWB, values, assets, income, housing, etc. Secondly, GNH index is used as weighted criterion in the allocation of budget among the local governments. Eight criteria are given prominence in the resource allocation formula to fund and mitigate deficient conditions, in a particular local government jurisdiction, like water and sanitation, or costly freight transport. Thirdly, policies in the central government are formulated by subjecting them to vetting with GNH policy screening tools, which consists of 22 criteria drawn from GNH and implemented according a well-defined process since 2008, revised further in 2015. So far, 15 out of 22 draft policies has been approved, with majority of them getting modified to some degree by the process of policy screening. Fourthly, GNH index has been used to evaluate a large rural horticultural project. In the fifth instance, GNH certification for business has been designed as an assessment framework for business corporations and its implementation is under way.

A glimpse of the changes in GNH index score between 2010 and 2015 shows us that performance in domains of health, education, culture, living standard, environment, time use, and good governance improved over this period, and hence, overall the GNH index improved. The index number improved only marginally: it was 0.743 in 2010 and it rose to 0.756 in 2015. The slow rate of change is a consequence of 277 variables some of which fall back in the course of broader movement forward. A comprehensive index is not necessarily parsimonious. And a comprehensive one like GNH attempts to take complexity into account instead of compelling us to declare victory by restricting our attention to a part of the battle where we fare well.

DASHO KARMA URA (Ph. D) is the President of the Center for Bhutan and GNH Studies, the main multidisciplinary think tank and research institution of the government of Bhutan. Its official mandates include GNH. Dasho Karma Ura has published many books, painted murals, and produced dances. In December 2006, His Majesty the Fourth King of Bhutan bestowed on him the honor of red scarf and the ancient title Dasho for his dedicated service to the country.

Origin of Happiness Policy Screening Tool

Bhutan was the first country to create a happiness screening tool, which they call their Gross National Happiness (GNH) Screening Tool.[1] In 2009, the Cabinet of Bhutan in 2008 adopted it to assess all policies under consideration, and grade each policy on a pass or fail basis.[2] Policies that have failed the screening process, for example, include joining the World Trade Organization and allowing strip mining and big dam energy projects.[3] The Cabinet of Bhutan also has a GNH Project Screening tool that contains many more aspects and is longer and more comprehensive than the GNH Policy Screening Tool. In Bhutan, the GNH Policy Screening tool was one of the first policies put in place with the transition from monarchy to democratic monarchy in 2008. The GNH Policy Screening took is updated periodically.[4]

The United Arab Emirates (UAE) was the second country to create a happiness screening tool, which they call the Happiness Screening Manual.[5] It was developed based on Bhutan's GNH Policy Screening tool. Their tool is used to guide policymakers as to what kind of policies to form as well as to evaluate policies under consideration. In the UAE, the policy screening tool was developed after the country began gathering happiness data.

POLICY HIGHLIGHT
Happiness as a Policy Parameter in Bhutan

by Kinga Tshering

As a former member of parliament, I used to represent my constituency of North Thimphu that includes that capital city of Bhutan that has around 6,500 registered voters, out of which 95 percent live in the city and the other 5 percent live in some of remotest highlands of the Jumolhari mountains. Since the early eighties, our King had foreseen that the highlands of Jumolhari would come under development pressure from an acceleration of the rural-urban migration of the highland youths drawn to the hustle and bustle of the towns. Compounding the problem, was the pressure from nomadic tribes from Tibet harvesting the cordyceps and grazing animals. To counter these pressures, years ago His Majesty decreed that the people of the highlands have the exclusive rights to collect cordyceps which fetch millions in the market. This stroke of genius has led to the high-landers having a new sense of wealth, pride, and ownership that has resulted in the protection of the pristine highland trekking paths, and the endangered species. Now, as politicians, while we do get questions of development in the highlands, the highlanders ensure that it is not at the cost of their cordyceps and natural environment.

This story may not be relevant to other countries or other contexts. My humble effort is to take inspiration and trace down the origin of GNH through our Great Fourth King, His Majesty Jigme Singye Wangchuk, when he famously propounded the vision of the GNH at the young age of sixteen. If now the economists and scholars can take any learning from these stories and develop a framework that can be applied elsewhere, then I will say that such policy tools are in line with our original concept of Bhutan's GNH.

KINGA TSHERING served in the public sector for twenty-three years in the Kingdom of Bhutan, most recently as the Member of Parliament in the National Assembly. He has experience in legislation, organization building with the formation of Bhutan Power Corporation (BPC), Bhutan Electricity Authority (BEA,) and Druk Holding and Investments (DHI). He also has experience in the financial sector, banking, energy, and infrastructure projects in the capacities of CEO and board member.

Instructions for Using the Happiness Policy Screening Tool

A model Happiness Policy Screening Tool can be found in Appendix J. It includes criteria for determining the impact on those who will be materially affected by a policy, program, or project under consideration. The criteria are based on the questions in the Happiness Alliance's Happiness Index.

Subjective indicators (i.e., survey questions) are paired with objective indicators sourced from the UN Sustainable Development Goal Indicators or the Organisation for Economic Co-operation and Development Better Life Index. In a few instances, the authors' expertise was used to identify objective indicators where such were lacking in the SDG indicators and OECD Better Life Index, such as for trust in businesses and government corruption and walkability for satisfaction with exercise.

The Happiness Policy Screening Tool we've provided can be adopted and modified, added to or simplified. When modifying it, it is important to ensure that sufficient criteria in all the domains of happiness are included so that assessments of happiness and well-being are meaningful. Happiness measurements as well as well-being, quality of life, and sustainability research can guide the modification of the Happiness Policy Screening Tool. Drawing from expertise of researchers and academics as well as members of a Happiness Council or other representatives from the Happiness Movement can also guide the modification of the Happiness Policy Screening Tool.

When using the Happiness Policy Screening Tool, it is important to note that all criteria count equally. For example, economic criteria do not outweigh social or environmental criteria. Thus, it is of particular importance when using the Happiness Policy Screening Tool that the criteria selected adequately reflect the spectrum of happiness domains.

The following steps are provided as guidelines for use of the Happiness Policy Screening Tool:

1. **Expert Committee.** Convene a committee of neutral experts in the domains of happiness that will be impacted. It is important that the experts who are on the committee are neutral and will not financially benefit from the outcome of the screening process or have a philosophical, reputational, or other kind of stake in the result.

2. **Criteria Selection.** The expert committee determines which criteria will be used for the screening process. Criteria should be selected that correspond to the nature of impacts within the domains of happiness. It is crucial that the range of impacts is

understood and that sufficient criteria are selected to cover this range.

3. **Criteria Grading.** Drawing from the expertise of the expert committee, each criterion should be assigned a value, with a value of one for a negative impact on stakeholders, two for an unknown impact, three for a neutral impact and four for a positive impact. It is important that sufficient assessment of the impacts has been conducted prior to performing this step.

4. **Screening Score.** The total number of criteria should be added. The sum of the grades for the criteria should be collected. The total number of criteria multiplied by the sum of grades is the final score. If the final score is three times the total number of criteria or above, then the policy passes the scoring and goes to policymakers to vote or otherwise make the decision about its promulgation. If it is below three times the total number of criteria, then the policy does not pass.

5. **Report to Decision Makers.** A report should be complied documenting the process for expert selection, stakeholders impact assessment, criteria selection, the rationale behind the grading process, and the final recommendation based on the score. This report should be provided to decision makers.

POLICY HIGHLIGHT

Engineering Action for a Flourishing Future

by John C. Havens

How will machines know what we value if we don't know ourselves?

The growing global focus on Artificial Intelligence governance demands that society define the values that we most want to imbue within the machines driving our future. Along with the specific design specifications data scientists and programmers must factor into the creation of AI, engineers writ large must provably demonstrate that what they're building is increasing human and environmental well-being and not only a single bottom line.

To that end, the Institute of Electrical and Electronics Engineers (IEEE, the world's largest technical professional organization) launched The IEEE Global Initiative on Ethics of Autonomous and Intelligent Systems (A/IS) in 2015 to create principles, guidelines, and inspire standards that could help ensure values-driven A/IS prioritize people and the planet along with profit.

To date, The IEEE Global Initiative has hosted a conference within the EU Parliament focusing on how AI governance would look if Beyond GDP Indicators were utilized in regards to its creation and use. Later in the same year, the second version of *Ethically Aligned Design: A Vision for Prioritizing Human Well-being for Autonomous and Intelligent Systems* was launched, featuring an entire chapter focused on the analysis of how A/IS technologies could be designed and utilized by aligning with Beyond GDP Indicators such as the OECD Better Life Index, Bhutan's Gross National Happiness, or the UN Sustainable Development Goals. This chapter further inspired the creation of a Standards Working Group called, IEEE P7010—Wellbeing Metrics Standard for Ethical Artificial Intelligence and Autonomous Systems. The standard establishes a baseline for the types of objective and subjective data A/IS should analyze and include in their programming and functioning to proactively increase human well-being.

Values alignment as a technical term means ensuring the robots and systems designed for a specific context or setting match predetermined outcomes A/IS creators wish to achieve. At a societal level, this practice is what the IEEE Global Initiative is emulating by the prioritization of triple-bottom-line design for A/IS. By educating the community building the machines and systems driving these technologies, we can promote a Well-being Policy Framework for A/IS that will engineer our flourishing future.

These thoughts represent John's views and do not necessarily represent any formal positions of IEEE, The IEEE Global Initiative, or CXI.

JOHN C. HAVENS is the executive director of the IEEE Global Initiative, executive director of The Council on Extended Intelligence (CXI). As executive director of the IEEE Global Initiative on Ethics of Autonomous and Intelligent Systems, John helps define guidelines for beneficial relationships between humans and their increasingly clever machine counterparts. His mission is to educate, train, and empower people involved with developing these future technologies in order to implement Ethically Aligned Design and improve outcomes for all. John is also executive director of the Council on Extended Intelligence (CXI), an interdisciplinary cohort of experts founded by the IEEE Standards Association and the MIT Media Lab that champions responsible participant design, data agency, and metrics of economic prosperity that prioritize people and the planet over profit and productivity. He has authored the books *Hacking Happiness* and *Heartificial Intelligence* in addition to contributing to Mashable and The Guardian. He also served as EVP of Social Media at Porter Novelli and spent a number of years as a professional actor.

Happiness Policy Screening Tool Scenario

For the sake of this scenario, imagine that steps have been taken so that a committee is ready to consider a policy aimed at improving living conditions for people living or working in their downtown. The committee has received a report of the Happiness Index scores for people living downtown compared to the general population in the city. In the figure below, the happiness data for people living downtown is depicted in the second column, and the score for the general population are in first column, with 0 as the worst possible and 100 as the best possible score. The scores show that downtown residents are hurting the most in the domain of community, with a score five points below the general population. They are also scoring lower than the general population in the domain of health and have low scores in the domain of time balance. See below for the sample scores.

The policy in question is to dedicate a half mile of a busy street in the downtown area to a pedestrian zone, allowing people to walk about one mile from end to end. Traffic would be rerouted to the streets directly adjacent and on either side of the area. Restaurants, cafés, and retail outlets would be allowed to use the sidewalks, and a craft and farmers market would be established and run by a local nonprofit that operates craft and farmers markets in other parts of the city. Construction costs to close the street to traffic would be minimal. Proponents are asking for daylighting of streams and the replacement of pavement with trees and greenery

	Scores for all people	Scores for a group
Cantril Ladder	70.3	68.1
Satisfaction with Life	69.4	67.9
Psychological Well-Being	70.9	70.6
Health	56.2	52.7
Time Balance	51.1	45.0
Community	50.6	45.6
Social Support	64.8	58.2
Lifelong Learning, Arts & Culture	65.5	69.2
Environment	66.3	54.3
Government	45.6	46.1
Standard of Living—Economy	68.8	70.2
Work	59.1	61.3

FIGURE 10.1. Scenario Happiness Data Report for people living downtown (second column) compared to general population (first column), on scale of 0–100, with 0 as the worst possible and 100 as the best possible score.

for strolling. No additional construction is planned. About half the retail owners are against the plan citing the decrease in parking spaces and lower visibility due to no car traffic passing their venues. Half the retailers and all of the restaurants and cafés are for it, eager for sidewalk seating and increased foot traffic. Public meetings reveal that most people are in favor, but some fear that the change will drive housing costs up. The committee has studied other areas that transformed streets into pedestrian zones and chosen twelve criteria and rated them based on research findings and expert opinion. Their findings indicate that there are impacts on satisfaction with life and happiness and in the domains of community, culture, environment, health, and standard of living and time balance. The committee has identified criteria from each domain and determined the score for each criteria. The score is in bold and has a check (✓) symbol after it.

■ Satisfaction with Life

SWL 1. Satisfaction with life.

Will decrease satisfaction with life.	Unknown impact on satisfaction with life.	Neutral impact on satisfaction with life.	Will increase satisfaction with life.
1	2	3	4 ✓

SWL 3. Sense of happiness.

Will decrease sense of happiness.	Unknown impact on sense of happiness.	Neutral impact on sense of happiness.	Will increase sense of happiness.
1	2	3	4 ✓

■ Health

H 6. Satisfaction with quality of exercise.

Will decrease satisfaction with quality of exercise.	Unknown impact on satisfaction with quality of exercise.	Neutral impact on satisfaction with quality of exercise.	Will increase satisfaction with quality of exercise.
1	2	3	4 √

■ Time Balance

TB 2. Leisure time spent with friends or family, or on hobbies or out of doors, away from home in previous 12 months.

Will decrease the amount of leisure time spent with friends or family, or on hobbies or out of doors.	Unknown impact on amount of leisure time spent with friends or family, or on hobbies or out of doors.	Neutral impact on amount of leisure time spent with friends or family, or on hobbies or out of doors.	Will increase the amount of leisure time spent with friends or family, or on hobbies or out of doors.
1	2	3	4 √

■ Community

C 1. Sense of belonging to a local community.

Will decrease sense of belonging to a local community.	Unknown impact on sense of belonging to a local community.	Neutral impact on sense of belonging to a local community.	Will increase sense of belonging to a local community.
1	2	3	4 √

C 5. Sense of trust in businesses in one's community.

Will decrease sense of trust in businesses in one's community.	Unknown impact on sense of trust in businesses in one's community.	Neutral impact on sense of trust in businesses in one's community.	Will increase sense of trust in businesses in one's community.
1	2	3 √	4

■ Lifelong Learning, Arts, and Culture

L 3. Creation of jobs and promotion of local culture and products through sustainable tourism.

Will decrease creation of jobs and promotion of local culture and products through sustainable tourism.	Unknown impact on creation of jobs and promotion of local culture and products through sustainable tourism.	Neutral impact on creation of jobs and promotion of local culture and products through sustainable tourism.	**Will increase creation of jobs and promotion of local culture and products through sustainable tourism.**
1	2	3	4 √

■ Environment

E 6. Satisfaction with opportunities to enjoy nature.

Will decrease satisfaction with opportunities to enjoy nature.	**Unknown impact on satisfaction with opportunities to enjoy nature.**	Neutral impact on satisfaction with opportunities to enjoy nature.	Will increase satisfaction with opportunities to enjoy nature.
1	2 √	3	4

E 7. Area of public and green space as a proportion of total town or city space.

Will decrease area of public and green space as a proportion of total city space.	Unknown impact on area of public and green space as a proportion of total city space.	Neutral impact on area of public and green space as a proportion of total city space.	**Will increase area of public and green space as a proportion of total city space.**
1	2	3	4 √

E 9. Greenhouse gas emissions and other air pollutant emissions.			
Will increase greenhouse gas emissions and other air pollutants.	Unknown impact on greenhouse gas emissions and other air pollutants.	Neutral impact on greenhouse gas emissions and other air pollutants.	Will decrease greenhouse gas emissions and other air pollutants.
1	2√	3	4

▪ Standard of Living/Personal Economy

EC 7. Access to safe, adequate, and nutritious food (i.e., Household Food Insecurity Access Scale — HFIAS) for measurement of food security in households across different cultural contexts.			
Will decrease access to safe, adequate, and nutritious food.	Unknown impact on access to safe, adequate, and nutritious food.	Neutral impact on access to safe, adequate, and nutritious food.	Will reduce access to safe, adequate, and nutritious food.
1	2√	3	4

EC 9. Household expenditure (cost of housing and maintenance of the house, water, energy, furnishings, etc.).			
Will increase household expenditure.	Unknown impact on household expenditure.	Neutral impact on household expenditure.	Will decrease household expenditure for well-being.
1√	2	3	4

The total number of factors considered is 12. A passing score would be 3 times the number of factors: 36. Anything below 36 would mean the policy does not pass.

In this case study, the total score is 38. The policy passes the screening test in this imaginary scenario. Once the policy is put in place, the Happiness Index can be used again to gather data for downtown residents and workers. If scores improve, then there

Domain	Criteria	Score
Satisfaction with life	Will increase satisfaction with life.	4
Satisfaction with life	Will increase sense of happiness.	4
Health	Will increase satisfaction with quality of exercise.	4
Time Balance	Will increase the amount of leisure time spent with friends or family, or on hobbies or out of doors.	4
Community	Will increase sense of belonging to a local community.	4
Community	Neutral impact on sense of trust in businesses in one's community.	3
Culture	Will increase creation of jobs and promotion of local culture and products through sustainable tourism.	4
Environment	Unknown impact on satisfaction with opportunities to enjoy nature.	2
Environment	Will increase area of public and green space as a proportion of total town or city space.	4
Environment	Unknown impact on greenhouse gas emissions and other air pollutants.	2
Standard of Living/ Personal Economy	Unknown impact on access to safe, adequate, and nutritious food	2
Standard of Living/ Personal Economy	Will increase household expenditure	1
	Total	38

may be some basis for assuming that the policy had a positive impact on the happiness and well-being of the target population.

If the total score had been less than 36, the committee may have decided to learn more about the impacts of the policy, or they may have decided to contemplate a different policy, depending on whether there were predominantly scores of two, for unknown impact, or one, for a negative impact.

This is an imaginary scenario. The Happiness Policy Screening Tool can be used in imaginary scenarios such as this one as a way to raise awareness and educate policymakers and the public about happiness tools for policy. It can also be adopted and adapted for use in screening policies by departments, committees, and other officials seeking to promulgate policies and institute programs and projects aimed at safeguarding people's happiness and communities' well-being.

POLICY HIGHLIGHT

On *The Origins of Happiness* and Policy Implications

by Sarah Flèche

As Thomas Jefferson once said, "The care of human life and happiness...is the only legitimate object of good government." But to make policy requires numbers. What is crucial in this respect is to lay out in quantitative terms how different factors such as income, education, employment, family conflict, health, childcare, and crime affect our life satisfaction, within one single framework. Our book, *The Origins of Happiness*, aims to provide this, using longitudinal data on over 100,000 individuals in Britain, the United States, Australia, and Germany (Clark et al., 2018). There are of course immediate influences (our current situation), but also more distant ones going back to our childhood, schooling, and family background.

We can start with the immediate causes. We have shown that the big factors explaining life satisfaction are all non-economic (whether someone is partnered, and especially how healthy they are). Less than two percent of the variance of life satisfaction is explained by income inequality. An obvious question is: do economic factors play a bigger role if we focus only on those who are the least happy (the bottom ten percent of the population in terms of life satisfaction)? When we investi-gate this, the results are almost the same as before. When we ask what distinguishes the least happy from the rest, the biggest distinguishing feature (other factors—such as income level, education level, employment status, and marriage status—being equal) is neither poverty, nor unemployment, but mental illness. And it explains more of the misery in the community than physical illness does.

Examining how childhood influences happiness in adulthood, we have shown that the best predictor of an adult's life satisfaction is their emotional health as a child, followed by their behavior. Academic performance is the least important predictor. This ranking is probably the inverse of that of most policymakers. The emotional health of the child is affected to some extent by family income but above all by the mother's mental health. The same is true of the child's behavior—which also affects the well-being of his or her surroundings. Schools matter as much as parents, and this applies equally to the academic performance of the pupils and to their happiness.

At last the map of happiness is becoming clearer and usable for policy analysis. We now need systematic evaluation of specific policies from which we can obtain estimates of the (causal) effect on life satisfaction in the near and longer term.

Reference

A. E. Clark, S. Flèche, R. Layard, N. Powdthavee, and G. Ward, *The Origins of Happiness: The Science of Well-being over the Life Course*, Princeton University Press, 2018.

SARAH FLÈCHE is a Research Associate at the London School of Economics' Centre for Economic Performance, where she worked as a full-time research officer between September 2014 and August 2017. She is also an assistant professor in economics at the Aix-Marseille School of Economics, in France. She previously worked as a consultant at the Organisation for Economic Co-operation and Development and completed her PhD in Economics at the Paris School of Economics in October 2014.

Closing

By now, you are likely inspired to move forward to help make the purpose of your government the happiness of the people who live there, but are wondering where to start. If you are ready and willing to take action, then the information you are about to read will help you chart your path even more clearly. On the other hand, if you are overwhelmed with the information or feel it was all too theoretical, we urge you to read on. The Appendices of this handbook contain hands-on insights, ideas, and plans that should help to clarify and inspire.

As with any change, uncertainties and unexpected things will always happen. Even trying to bring attention and focus to the need for embedding happiness within governance may result in some change, whether incremental and small or more immediate and with larger impact. Sometimes, by focusing attention on what is wanted, others become inspired to join your efforts. There is synergy in bringing people together to discuss and activate interests, and as presented throughout this handbook, many ways to do this exist.

We have covered much in this journey of sharing insights and ideas with you about happiness policy. From its origins to its foundations rooted in economics, psychology, and health, happiness as policy and as a movement has been explored in the first section.

We hope this has provided you with a grounding and understanding of what happiness policy is and why it should be of concern for governments and those governed by them. The Appendices shift our focus to a very applied orientation, with action plans to implement. From a happiness proclamation to engagement tools, this section also includes ways to measure happiness. It is critical to measure happiness so, as it is hard to gauge progress towards goals without measuring what will aid in assessment and evaluation.

It is our sincere hope that this handbook will enable and empower you to pursue happiness, both for yourself and others in your community, region, and/or nation. By focusing on policy, definitive action can be taken, and via that action, desired results can be achieved for your area. We encourage you to reach out to others in the happiness movement for support and sharing of ideas. Additionally, ask others to join you in learning more and implementing policies to achieve happiness and well-being in ways that will empower all with opportunities to flourish.

Concept Menu
of Happiness Policies

The policies, programs, and projects listed in this appendix have been implemented by governments. Alongside explanations are links to example ordinances, plans, and other documentation. The policies provided in this section are suggestions for starting places. Every area has its own unique circumstances and the needs of different populations vary considerably. There is no one-size fits-all policy that will increase happiness for every person. Instead, to understand what policies will increase happiness it is important to understand where people perceive themselves to be thriving and where they perceive themselves to be hurting. To understand whether a policy once implemented has increased happiness and well-being, it is important to have a baseline, and to measure the impact compared to the baseline. This can be done with happiness measurements.

Happiness Policies in the Domain of Community
Sustainable Community Development

Mark Roseland, *Toward Sustainable Communities: Solutions for Citizens and Their Governments*, New Society Publishers, 2012.

Rhonda Phillips, Bruce Seifer, and Ed Antczak, *Sustainable Communities: Creating a Durable Local Economy*, Routledge, 2013.

What Is a Sustainable Community? The Star Community Rating System defines sustainable communities: starcommunities.org/education /principles

Sustainable Communities Online provides information about sustainable community formation: sustainable.org

Community Centers

Partners for Livable Communities offers Best Practices from communities across the USA: livable.org/livability-resources/best-practices

Infed (a not-for-profit site provided by the YMCA George Williams
    College) has a page called *Community centres (centers) and associa-
    tions: their history, theory, development and practice.* infed.org/mobi
    /community-centers-and-associations
The American Association of Retired Persons (AARP) reports on
    America's Best Intergenerational Communities. aarp.org/livable
    -communities/learn/civic-community/info-12-2012/americas-best
    -intergenerational-communities.html
The Sonoma County Department of Health Services Report (2012): Best
    Practices in Action Strategies for Engaging Latinos, Seniors and Low-
    Income Residents of Sonoma County. sonoma-county.org/health
    /community/pdf/report.pdf

Departments of Neighborhoods

City of Seattle's Department of Neighborhoods: seattle.gov
    /neighborhoods
City of Houston's Department of Neighborhoods: houstontx.gov
    /neighborhoods
Jim Diers, *Seattle's Department of Neighborhoods: Enhancing Government
    Effectiveness by Empowering Communities.* courses.washington.edu
    /quanzhou/pacrim/papers/Diers-China_Paper.pdf

Village Living

Port Townsend's Mixed-Use Zoning Districts: codepublishing.com
    /WA/PortTownsend/html/PortTownsend17/PortTownsend1718
    .html
Metropolitan Boston Area Planning, *Mixed-Use Zoning: A Planners'
    Guide.* mapc.org/wp-content/uploads/2017/11/Mixed_Use_Planners
    _Toolkit.pdf

Volunteerism Programs

City of Red Deer's toolkit *Building Public Awareness.* reddeer.ca/media
    /reddeerca/recreation-and-culture/community-programs-and
    -information/Public-Awareness-Toolkit.pdf
50 Stealable Grassroots Marketing Campaigns by Ann Dermody.
    info.cq.com/resources/50-grassroots-marketing-campaign-examples/
City of Sacramento's webpage *Volunteer Opportunities:* cityofsacramento
    .org/HR/Volunteer-Opportunities

Transforming Streets into Public Spaces

Project for Public Spaces, *Ten Strategies for Transforming Cities and Public Spaces Through Placemaking.* pps.org/reference/ten-strategies-for-transforming-cities-through-placemaking-public-spaces

Smart Growth America and National Complete Streets Coalition's report: *Safer Streets, Stronger Economies.* smartgrowthamerica.org/app/uploads/2016/08/safer-streets-stronger-economies.pdf

City of Charlotte's *Appendix Mobile Grocery Store Research Copies of City Ordinances and Regulations.* charmeck.org/Planning/Rezoning/MobileFoodVendors/MobileFoodUnitOrdinances.pdf

City of Conley's *Buskers Permit Application.* cityofconway.com/Buskers%20Permit%20Application.pdf

City of Boston's *Food Truck Legal Toolkit.* chlpi.org//wp-content/uploads/2013/12/12.18.13-Full-Food-Truck-Legal-Toolkit.pdf

City of San Francisco's *Block Parties and Street Fairs.* sfbetterstreets.org/find-project-types/activating-street-space/block-parties-and-street-fairs/

Happiness Policies in the Domain of Economy

Housing security

Mental Health Commission of Canada and the Homeless Hub, *Canadian Housing First Toolkit.* housingfirsttoolkit.ca and homelesshub.ca/solutions/housing-first/canadian-housing-first-toolkit

City of Victoria, *British Columbia's Victoria Cool Aid Society shelter, housing, and community service program.* ighhub.org/sites/default/files/CoolAid_0.pdf

City of Richmond, *Rent Control Ordinance* No. 21-15 N.S. ci.richmond.ca.us/ArchiveCenter/ViewFile/Item/6688

New Brunswick, *Rent Control in Plain Language Summary.* thecityofnewbrunswick.org/planninganddevelopment/wp-content/uploads/sites/8/2011/09/2017-Rent-Control-Plain-Language-Summary-English.pdf

Scott Carrier, *The Shockingly Simple, Surprisingly Cost-Effective Way to End Homelessness, Mother Jones,* February 17, 2015. motherjones.com/politics/2015/02/housing-first-solution-to-homelessness-utah

Food Security Programs

City of Vancouver, British Columbia, *Food and sustainable food systems.* vancouver.ca/people-programs/food.aspx

Ottawa Food Policy Council, *Community Programming for Food Security, Food Education and Awareness.* ofpc-cpao.ca/ottawa-food-action-plan /community-programming-for-food-security-food-education-and -awareness

World Future Council, *Celebrating the Belo Horizonte Food Security Programme.* worldfuturecouncil.org/wp-content/uploads/2016/01 /WFC_2009_Future_Policy_Award.pdf

FoodShare's *How To Guides* for starting community gardens: foodshare .net/resources/printable/

Food Desert Elimination

Foodtank, *Five Innovative Solutions from "Food Desert" Activists.* foodtank .com/news/2013/05/five-innovative-solutions-from-food-desert -activists/

Food Secure Canada, *Five Big Ideas for a Better Food System.* foodsecure canada.org/policy-advocacy/five-big-ideas-better-food-system

Sarah Corapi, *Why it takes more than a grocery store to eliminate a "food desert."* pbs.org/newshour/updates/takes-grocery-store-eliminate -food-desert/

EfficientGov Staff, *Getting Rid of Food Deserts.* efficientgov.com/blog /2015/05/12/getting-rid-of-food-deserts

Sarah Parsons, *Just Deserts: 6 Ways to Bring Food to Poor Neighborhoods How to End Food Deserts and Bring Healthy Food to Poor Neighbor- hoods.* good.is/articles/just-deserts-6-ways-to-bring-good-food-to -poor-neighborhoods

Tax Incentives for Savings for Low and Middle Income

Karen Dynan, *Better Ways to Promote Saving through the Tax System.* brookings.edu/research/better-ways-to-promote-saving-through-the -tax-system/

M. Greenstone, M. Harris, et al., eds., *15 Ways to Rethink the Federal Budget,* (See p. 36 for Proposal 6: Better Ways to Promote Saving through the Tax System). hamiltonproject.org/assets/legacy/files /downloads_and_links/THP_15WaysRethinkFedDeficit_Feb13 _rev_1.pdf

Progressive Tax Rates

Joseph E. Stiglitz, *Reforming Taxation to Promote Growth and Equity.* rooseveltinstitute.org/wp-content/uploads/2014/05/Stiglitz _Reforming_Taxation_White_Paper_Roosevelt_Institute.pdf

Tax Foundation, *U.S. Federal Individual Income Tax Rates History, 1862–2013 (Nominal and Inflation-Adjusted Brackets)*. taxfoundation.org /us-federal-individual-income-tax-rates-history-1913-2013-nominal -and-inflation-adjusted-brackets

Marc Lee, *Fighting poverty through tax credit reform*. policynote.ca/fighting -poverty-through-tax-credit-reform/

Toby Sanger, *A Crisis of Public Revenue*. policyalternatives.ca/publications /monitor/crisis-public-revenue

Guaranteed Basic Income

OECD Policy Brief, *Basic income as a policy option: can it add up?* oecd.org /social/Basic-Income-Policy-Option-2017.pdf

Basic Income Earth Network (BIEN), *About basic income*. basicincome .org/basic-income

Hugh Segal, *A universal basic income in Canada is more realistic than you think*. macleans.ca/opinion/a-basic-universal-income-in-canada-is -more-realistic-than-you-think/

College Debt Forgiveness Program

Natalia Abrams and Cody Hounanian, *5 Countries that Know How to Handle Student Debt*. thenation.com/article/five-countries-that-know -how-to-handle-student-debt/

European Commission, EACEA, *National Student Fee and Support Systems in European Higher Education 2017/2018*. eacea.ec.europa.eu /erasmus-plus/news/new-eurydice-publication-national-student-fee -and-support-systems-in-european-higher-education_en

Limits on Interest Rates Charged by Credit Companies

LoanBack, *Usury Laws by State*. loanback.com/category/usury-laws-by -state/

Robert E. Litan, *Proposed Limits on ATM Fees and Credit Card Interest Rates: Counter-Productive Punishment That Goes Too Far*. brookings .edu/research/proposed-limits-on-atm-fees-and-credit-card-interest -rates-counter-productive-punishment-that-goes-too-far/

Green Energy Development

Department of Energy's *Template Solar Energy Development* at energy.gov /savings/template-solar-energy-development-ordinance

American Planning Association, *Planning and Zoning for Solar Energy*. planning.org/pas/infopackets/eip30.htm

Kabir Nadkarni and Sara Hastings-Simon, Pembina Institute, *Alberta Community Solar Guide*. pembina.org/pub/alberta-community-solar-guide

Pembina Institute, *Community-Owned Renewables Fact Sheet*. pembina.org/reports/community-owned-re-fact-sheet.pdf

Zero Waste Goals

City of Boulder, Colorado's *Universal Zero Waste Ordinance*. bouldercolorado.gov/zero-waste/universal-zero-waste-ordinance

US Environmental Protection Agency, *Zero Waste Case Study: San Francisco*. epa.gov/transforming-waste-tool/zero-waste-case-study-san-francisco

Zero Food Waste at Groceries and Restaurants

Massachusetts Department of Environmental Protection Guide, *Commercial Food Material Disposal Ban*. mass.gov/guides/commercial-food-material-disposal-ban

State of California, CalRecycle, Food Scraps Management: Organic Materials Management. calrecycle.ca.gov/organics/food

Corin Cook, *Local grocery stores innovating food waste disposal*. washingtontimes.com/news/2016/jul/18/local-grocery-stores-innovating-food-waste-disposa/

Angelique Chrisafis, *French law forbids food waste in supermarkets*. theguardian.com/world/2016/feb/04/french-law-forbids-food-waste-by-supermarkets

Tahiat Mahboob, *Wasted! The Story of Food Waste*. cbc.ca/passionateeye/features/15-canadian-initiatives-trying-to-reduce-food-waste

Closed Loop Systems

State of California Department of Justice, *State and Local Government Green Building Ordinances* in California. ag.ca.gov/globalwarming/pdf/green_building.pdf

EPA *Green Building Tools for Tribes*. epa.gov/green-building-tools-tribes

EPA *Tools and Resources for Sustainable Communities*. epa.gov/smartgrowth/tools-and-resources-sustainable-communities

Swedish Energy Agency, *District Heating*. energimyndigheten.se/en/sustainability/households/heating-your-home/district-heating/

The London Plan, *Chapter Five: London's Response to Climate Change*. london.gov.uk/what-we-do/planning/london-plan/current-london-plan/london-plan-chapter-five-londons-response-poli-0

Scottish and Southern Energy, *Greenwatt Way Project.* sse.co.uk/help
/energy/energy-efficiency/greenwatt-way

Circular Economies

Think Denmark, *Circular Economy: Denmark as a circular economy solution
hub.* stateofgreen.com/files/download/10574
Example Policy:
World Bank Group, *China Circular Economy Promotion Law.* ppp.world
bank.org/public-private-partnership/library/china-circular-economy
-promotion-law
European Commission, *Circular Economy Action Plan.* ec.europa.eu
/futurium/en/circular-economy/circular-economy-final-action-plan
-now-available-0

Blockchain

Michael Crosby et al., *Blockchain Technology Beyond Bitcoin* scet.berkeley
.edu/wp-content/uploads/BlockchainPaper.pdf
Cade Morgan and Margaret A. Mentz, *Blockchain and State Law: Five
Legislative Developments.* bakerdonelson.com/blockchain-and-state
-law-five-legislative-developments
Luke Parker, *Ukraine to use blockchain technology in curtailing corruption
when selling government assets.* bravenewcoin.com/news/ukraine-to
-use-blockchain-technology-in-curtailing-corruption-when-selling
-government-assets/

Happiness Policies in the Domain of Environment
Comprehensive Planning that Includes Planning for Climate Change

US Environmental Protection Agency, Climate Change Adaptation Resource Center, *Planning for Climate Change Adaptation.* epa.gov/arc-x
/planning-climate-change-adaptation
Adaptation Clearinghouse, *California General Plan Guidelines.*
adaptationclearinghouse.org/resources/california-general-plan-guide
lines.html

Conservation Programs

Friends of Ridgefield National Wildlife Refuge, *Urban Wildlife Conservation Program.* ridgefieldfriends.org/urban-wildlife-conservation
-program/
European Union, *Restoring Europe's Rivers.* restorerivers.eu/wiki/index
.php?title=Main_Page

US Department of Agriculture and US Forest Service, *Urban Wildlife.*
   fs.fed.us/research/urban/wildlife/

Daylighting Urban Streams

European Centre for River Restoration Case Study: Cheonggyecheon
   Restoration Project. ecrr.org/Portals/27/Cheonggyecheon%20case%20
   study.pdf
American Rivers, *Daylighting Streams: Breathing Life into Urban Streams
   and Communities.* americanrivers.org/conservation-resource
   /daylighting-streams-breathing-life-urban-streams-communities/

Green Urban Growth Ordinance

Oregon Metro, *Urban growth boundary.* oregonmetro.gov/urban-growth
   -boundary
Jacques Cousteau National Estuarine Research Reserve, *Urban Sprawl.*
   rucore.libraries.rutgers.edu/rutgers-lib/17657/PDF/1

Building and Expanding Open Spaces, Parks, and Fields in Urban Areas

City of New Orleans, *Master Plan City Park 2018.* neworleanscitypark
   .com/info/master-plan-city-park-2018
City of Santa Monica, *Parks and Recreation Master Plan.* smgov.net
   /uploadedFiles/Departments/CCS/Places_Parks_Beach/Parks
   /Parks_and_Recreation_Master_Plan.pdf
City of St. Paul's Parks and Recreation. stpaul.gov/departments/parks
   -recreation
City of Boulder Conservation Easements. bouldercounty.org/open-space
   /management/conservation-easements/

Urban Tree Program

City of Vancouver, *Urban Forestry.* cityofvancouver.us/publicworks/page
   /urban-forestry
City of Portland Tree Canopy program. portlandoregon.gov/parks/60401

Public Transportation

Victoria Transport Policy Institute, *Public Transit Encouragement.* vtpi.org
   /tdm/tdm112.htm
European Commission, *Increasing peoples' awareness and use of public
   transport through active mobility consultancy with focus on feeder systems
   (SmartMove).* ec.europa.eu/energy/intelligent/projects/en/projects
   /smartmove

C. Cheong and N. Loh, *Transport Policies and Patterns: A Comparison of Five Asian Cities*. slidex.tips/download/transport-policies-and -patterns-a-comparison-of-five-asian-cities

Stefan Gossling, *Urban Transport Transitions: Copenhagen, City of Cyclists*. researchgate.net/publication/259138837_Urban_transport_transitions _Copenhagen_City_of_Cyclists

Happiness Policies in the Domain of Government

Voter Turnout

Australian Electoral Commission, *Compulsory Voting*. aec.gov.au/Voting /Compulsory_Voting.htm

Employment New Zealand, *General Election Voting Leave*. employment.govt .nz/leave-and-holidays/other-types-of-leave/election-voting-leave/

International Institute for Democracy and Electoral Assistance, *What Is Compulsory Voting?* idea.int/data-tools/data/voter-turnout /compulsory-voting

Anti-Corruption Policies

Southampton City Council, *Anti-fraud and anti-corruption policy and strategy*. southampton.gov.uk/council-democracy/corp-governance /antifraud-anticorruption-strategy.aspx

Elizabeth Andreson, The International Centre for Criminal Law Reform and Criminal Justice Policy, *Municipal "Best Practices": Preventing Fraud, Bribery and Corruption*. icclr.law.ubc.ca/publication/municipal -best-practices-preventing-fraud-bribery-and-corruption/

Kingsley Dennis, *Keeping a Close Watch—The Rise of Self-Surveillance & the Threat of Digital Exposure*. quigley.mab.ms/wp-content/uploads /2012/01/Keeping-a-Close-Watch-The-Rise-of-Self-Surveillance -KD-version.pdf

Transparency in Government Programs

Transparency International, *Campaign for Transparency in Maldives Pays Off*. blog.transparency.org/2014/07/10/campaign-for-transparency -in-maldives-pays-off/

Transparency Accountability Initiative, *Open Government—Local Government*. transparency-initiative.org/archive/news/open-government -local-government

Government Technology, *Open Data Policies in State and Local Government (Interactive Map)*. govtech.com/data/Are-Governments -Committed-to-Open-Data-Interactive-Map.html

E-Identity Cards

e-estonia, Estonia's e-identify card program. e-estonia.com/solutions
/e-identity/

World Economic Forum White Paper, *Digital Identity On the Threshold
of a Digital Identity Revolution* weforum.org/docs/White_Paper
_Digital_Identity_Threshold_Digital_Identity_Revolution_report
_2018.pdf

Campaign Finance Reform

League of California Cities, *A Primer on Local Campaign Finance Reform
Ordinances.* cacities.org/getattachment/bc330c98-c09f-436e-a77c-a2
f8b1cf74bc/2-2008-Local-Campaign-Finance-Reform-Pras

BallotPedia. *Campaign Finance Regulation.* ballotpedia.org/Campaign
_finance_regulation

Participatory Governance

Civicus, *Participatory Governance Toolkit.* civicus.org/index.php/es
/centro-de-medios/recursos/manuales/611-participatory-governance-
toolkit

Organization for Security and Co-operation in Europe, *Guide to Municipal Participatory Governance.* osce.org/kosovo/31771

Silvia Suteu, *Constitutional Conventions in the Digital Era: Lessons from
Iceland and Ireland* (p. 260–264). lawdigitalcommons.bc.edu/cgi/view
content.cgi?article=1748&context=iclr

Brian Walper and Stephanie L. McNulty, *Does Participatory Governance
Matter? Exploring the Nature and Impact of Participatory Reforms.*
wilsoncenter.org/sites/default/files/CUSP_110108_Participatory%20
Gov.pdf

E. Turnhout, S. Van Bommell, and N. Aarts, *How Participation Creates
Citizens: Participatory Governance as Performative Practice.* ecologyand
society.org/vol15/iss4/art26/

Participatory Budgeting

City of Cambridge, *Participatory Budgeting.* cambridgema.gov/Services
/participatorybudgeting

Participatory Budgeting Project. participatorybudgeting.org/

Camilla Hansen, *What Would Real Democracy Look Like?* roarmag.org
/essays/real-direct-participatory-democracy/

Compassion Training for Police

Ari Cowan, International Center for Compassionate Organizations, *The Impact of Police Compassion Competency*. compassionate.center/docs /WP-The_Impact_of_Police_Compassion_Competency.pdf

International Association of Police Chiefs, *Officer Safety Corner: Compassion in Law Enforcement*. policechiefmagazine.org/officer-safety -corner-compassion-in-law-enforcement/

Happiness Policies in the Domain of Health

Walkable Cities

Mid-America Regional Council, *Creating Walkable Communities*. bikewalk.org/pdfs/ncbwpubwalkablecomm.pdf

Peggy Edwards and Agis D. Tsouros, World Health Organization, *A Healthy City Is an Active City*. euro.who.int/__data/assets/pdf _file/0012/99975/E91883.pdf

Urban Agriculture

City of Seattle *Ordinance 123378 for Urban Farms and Community Gardens*. clerk.ci.seattle.wa.us/search/ordinances/123378

National Policy and Legal Analysis Network to Prevent Childhood Obesity and Change Lab Solutions, *Seeding the City: Land Use Policies to Promote Urban Agriculture*: changelabsolutions.org/publications /seeding-city

American Planning Association, *Urban Agriculture*. planning.org /knowledgebase/urbanagriculture/

Farmers Markets

Planning for Healthy Places Project, Public Health Law and Policy, *Establishing Land Use Protection for Farmer's Markets*. michigan.gov /documents/mdch/Farmers_Markets_3-09_Public_Health_Law _Policy_303375_7.pdf

Farmer Market Coalition, *Federal Policies & Programs*. farmersmarket coalition.org/advocacy/policy-priorities/

BC Association of Farmers Markets. bcfarmersmarket.org/

Bike Friendly Cities and Towns

The League of American Bicyclists, *Model Legislation*. bikeleague.org /content/model-legislation-0

Initiative for Healthy Infrastructure, *Planning and Policy Models for Pedestrian and Bicycle Friendly Communities in New York State.* albany.edu /ihi/files/NY_Planning_And_Policy_Models_iHi.pdf

Oregon Bicycle and Pedestrian Plan – Issues and Opportunities Report 2014. library.state.or.us/repository/2014/201409111335224/index.pdf

Importance of Sleep Awareness-Raising Campaign

G. Perry, S. Patil, and L. Presley-Cantrell, Centers for Disease Control and Prevention, *Raising Awareness of Sleep as a Healthy Behavior.* cdc .gov/pcd/issues/2013/13_0081.htm

American Academy of Sleep Medicine, *National Healthy Sleep Awareness Project.* sleepeducation.org/healthysleep

Happiness Policies in the Domain of Lifelong Learning, Arts, and Culture

Happiness Education in Public Schools

R. Ijadi-Maghsoodi, L. Marlott, et al., *Adapting and Implementing a School-Based Resilience-Building Curriculum Among Low-Income Racial and Ethnic Minority Students.* ncbi.nlm.nih.gov/pmc/articles /PMC5909715/

R. Crane and W. Kuyken, *The Implementation of Mindfulness-Based Cognitive Therapy: Learning From the UK Health Service Experience.* link.springer.com/article/10.1007/s12671-012-0121-6

Adult Literacy Programs

City of Philadelphia, Office of Adult Education. philaliteracy.org/

A. Lesgold and M.Welch-Ross, *Improving Adult Literacy Instruction: Options for Practice and Research.* ride.ri.gov/Portals/0/Uploads /Documents/Students-and-Families-Great-Schools/Educational -Programming/Adult-Education-Standards/Improving-Adult -Literacy-Instruction-Research-report.pdf

Lifelong Learning Programs

Quebec City's *Lifelong Learning Program.* lifelonglearningquebec.org

City of San Diego Public Library, *Adult Education.* sandiego.gov/public -library/services/adulteducation

Low-Cost or Tuition-Free College

Tennessee Promise, *Tuition-Free Program.* tennesseepromise.gov/about .shtml

Demos, *The Affordable College Compact.* demos.org/publication
/affordable-college-compact

Educational Institutions in Rural and Economically Depressed Areas

MDC, *Expanding Economic and Educational Opportunity in Distressed
Rural Areas: A Conceptual Framework for the Rural Community
College Initiative.* mdcinc.org/expanding-economic-and-educational
-opportunity-in-distressed-rural-areas/

City of Roanoke, Virginia, *Creating a Biomedical Research Facility and
Technical Park* in EPA report *How Small Towns and Cities Can Use
Local Assets to Rebuild Their Economies: Lessons from Successful Places.*
epa.gov/sites/production/files/2015-05/documents/competitive
_advantage_051215_508_final.pdf

Culture and Creativity Programs

City of Sydney, *Cultural Policy and Action Plan.* cityofsydney.nsw.gov.
au/vision/towards-2030/communities-and-culture/culture-and
-creativity

Charles Landry, *Creativity, Culture & the City: A question of interconnec-
tion.* forum-avignon.org/sites/default/files/editeur/ECCE_report.pdf

Bernard Momer, *The Creative Sector in Kelowna, British Columbia: an
economic impact assessment.* kelowna.ca/sites/files/1/docs/community
/2010_ac_eia_final.pdf

Protection of Heritage Sites

Tennessee Historical Commission, *Tennessee Heritage Protection Act.*
tn.gov/environment/about-tdec/tennessee-historical-commission/
redirect---tennessee-historical-commission/tennessee-heritage
-protection-act.html

UNESCO World Heritage Convention, *Examples of the Convention at
Work.* whc.unesco.org/en/casestudies/

Happiness Policies in the Domain of Social Support

Parental Support Programs

City of Santa Clara, California, *Parents.* santaclaraca.gov/residents
/children-youth-teens/santa-clara-0-to-6/parents

City of Loveland, Colorado, *Parenting Resources.* ci.loveland.co.us/depart
ments/police/community-resources/school-resources/parenting
-resources

Age-Friendly Cities

World Health Organization, *Global Age-Friendly Cities: A Guide* (checklists on pages 17 and 18). who.int/ageing/publications/Global_age
_friendly_cities_Guide_English.pdf?ua=1

Natalie Turner, AARP, *Age-Friendly: The 2014 World Tour*. aarp.org
/livable-communities/info-2014/age-friendly-world-tour.html

Public Day Care

Inge Schreyer and Pamela Oberhuemer, *Denmark Key Contextual Data*.
seepro.eu/English/pdfs/DENMARK_Key_Data.pdf

OECD, *Early Childhood Education and Care Policy in Denmark*. oecd.org
/education/school/2475168.pdf

FAO Trade and Labour, *Family Day-Care in Denmark* (see page 17–21 on
legislation) applikationer.foa.dk/publikationer/pjecer/Paedagogisk
/FamilyDayCareInDenmark.pdf

Intergenerational Care

Sherbrooke Community Centre, Saskatoon, Saskatchewan. *Intergenerational Care Program*. sherbrookecommunitycentre.ca/about
-sherbrooke/igen-intergenerational-classroom/

Babies At Work, *Resources*. babiesatwork.org/resources

Generations United. gu.org

AARP, *America's Best Intergenerational Communities*. aarp.org/livable
-communities/learn/civic-community/info-12-2012/americas-best
-intergenerational-communities.html

Same-Sex Marriage Laws

Canadian Government *Civil Marriage Act S.C. 2005, c. 33*. laws-lois.justice
.gc.ca/eng/acts/c-31.5/page-1.html

The Williams Institute, UCLA School of Law, *Same-Sex Couples and
Marriage: Model Legislation for Allowing Same-Sex Couples to Marry
or All Couples to Form a Civil Union*. williamsinstitute.law.ucla.edu
/research/marriage-and-couples-rights/pizer-kuehl-model-marriage
-civil-union-code-aug-2012

Loneliness Awareness Raising Campaigns

Campaign to End Loneliness. campaigntoendloneliness.org

Center for the Study of Social Policy, *Strengthening Families: Social Connections*. cssp.org/wp-content/uploads/2018/08/SF_Social-Connections
.pdf

AARP, *Framework for Isolation in Adults over 50.* aarp.org/content/dam/
aarp/aarp_foundation/2012_PDFs/AARP-Foundation-Isolation
-Framework-Report.pdf

Happiness Policies in the Domain of Psychological Well-Being
Mental Health Care

National Alliance on Mental Illness, *Engagement: A New Standard for
Mental Health Care.* nami.org/engagement

World Health Organization, *Improving Health Systems and Services for
Mental Health.* who.int/mental_health/policy/services/mhsystems/en/

Compassion Awareness Campaigns

Charter for Compassion, *Participating Communities.* charterforcompassion
.org/communities/participating-communities#affirmed-the-charter

Compassionate Games, *Survival of the Kindest.* compassiongames.org

Bans on Advertising to Children

Advertising Standards Authority, *Children and Young People's Advertising
Code.* asa.co.nz/codes/codes/new-children-young-peoples-advertising
-code

Library of European Parliament, *Protection of Minors in the Media Environment.* europarl.europa.eu/RegData/bibliotheque/briefing/2013
/130462/LDM_BRI(2013)130462_REV1_EN.pdf

Melissa Dittmann, American Psychological Association, *Protecting Children from Advertising.* apa.org/monitor/jun04/protecting.aspx

UK House of Commons Briefing Paper CBP08198, *Advertising to Children* (pages 8–11). researchbriefings.files.parliament.uk/documents
/CBP-8198/CBP-8198.pdf

Child-Friendly City Ordinances

Japan for Sustainability, *Nara City Enacts Child-Friendly City Ordinance.*
japanfs.org/en/news/archives/news_id035231.html

UNICEF Child Friendly Cities Initiative. childfriendlycities.org/

Happiness Policies in the Domain of Time Balance
Vacation, Sick Leave, and Family Leave Laws

Paid Sick Days. paidsickdays.org

National Conference of State Legislatures, *State Family and Medical Leave
Laws.* ncsl.org/research/labor-and-employment/state-family-and
-medical-leave-laws.aspx

Flex Time, Job Sharing, and Telecommuting

Manitoba Civil Service Commission, *Job Sharing And/Or Part-Time Work Arrangements Guidelines*. gov.mb.ca/csc/pdf/jobshare.pdf

California Department of Human Resources, *Telework Policy*. calhr.ca.gov /employees/Pages/telework-policy.aspx

Workforce, *Sample Flextime Policy*. workforce.com/2002/09/05/sample -flextime-policy/

Personal Holidays

City of Portland Human Resources Administrative Rules document 6.02, *Holidays* (bottom of page 3, personal holidays). portlandoregon.gov /citycode/?c=27938&a=12412

City of Madison Human Resources, *Vacation & Holidays* (scroll down to personal holidays). cityofmadison.com/human-resources/benefits /vacation-holidays

Part-Time Work

Jan Hendeliowitz, Danish National Labour Market Authority, *Danish Employment Policy*. oecd.org/employment/leed/40575308.pdf

electronic Irish Statute Book. *Protection of Employees (Part-Time Work) Act, 2001*. irishstatutebook.ie/eli/2001/act/45/enacted/en/html

Happiness Policies in the Domain of Work

Job Placement Programs

City of Minneapolis, Community Planning & Economic Development, *Minneapolis Employment and Training*. ci.minneapolis.mn.us/cped /metp/index.htm

Robert P. Giloth, Annie E. Casey Foundation, *Lessons for a New Context: Workforce Development in an Era of Economic Challenge*. frbsf.org /community-development/files/Giloth_Robert.pdf

United States Interagency Council on Homelessness, *Partnership for Opening Doors*. usich.gov/resources/uploads/asset_library/Partner ship_Summit_Effective_Practices.pdf

Job Security Programs

OECD, *Danish Employment Policy*. oecd.org/employment/leed/40575308 .pdf

Eurofound, *Denmark: New Reform Targets Unemployment*. eurofound .europa.eu/publications/article/2014/denmark-new-reform-targets -unemployment

Part Time Work And Job Sharing

UK Civil Service Employee Policy, *Guide to Job Sharing*. assets.publishing
.service.gov.uk/government/uploads/system/uploads/attachment
_data/file/406045/JobShareGuide260115FVnoDNs.pdf

Entrepreneurship

City of Austin. *Small Business Incentives Guide*. austintexas.gov/sites
/default/files/files/EGRSO/Small_Business_Incentive_Guide.pdf
Nate Baker, *Tybee Island Small Business Incentive Program*. digitalcommons
.georgiasouthern.edu/cgi/viewcontent.cgi?referer=&httpsredir=1
&article=1010&context=gma_practicum

Innovation Hubs

City of Philadelphia, Center City District, *Innovation Hub*. centercityphila
.org/doing-business/why-center-city/innovation-hub
Ian Hathaway, Brookings Institute, *Accelerating Growth: Startup Accelera-
tor Programs in the United States*. brookings.edu/research/accelerating
-growth-startup-accelerator-programs-in-the-united-states/

Street Vendors

Yale Law School, Transnational Development Clinic, *Working Paper
Developing National Street Vendor Legislation in India: A Compar-
ative Study of Street Vending Regulation*. law.yale.edu/system/files
/documents/pdf/Clinics/TDC_ComparativeStudyStreetVending.pdf
Women in Informal Employment: Globalizing and Organizing, *Street
Vendors and the Law*. wiego.org/informal_economy_law/street
-vendors-and-law
New York City, *General Street Vendor License*. nyc.gov/nyc-resources
/service/2938/general-street-vendor-license

Worker Councils

European Union Directive 2002/14/EC, *Establishing a general framework for informing and consulting employees in the European Community*. eur-lex.europa.eu/legal-content/EN/TXT/?qid=1497141683
067&uri=CELEX:32002L0014
Roy J. Adams, Bureau of Labor Statistics, *Should works councils be used as
industrial relations policy?* bls.gov/opub/mlr/1985/07/art4full.pdf
M. Finkin and T. Kochan, *The Volkswagen way to better labor-management
relations*. articles.latimes.com/2014/jan/20/opinion/la-oe-finkin-vw
-work-councils-20140120

Cooperative Corporate Formation

United States Department of Agriculture Rural Development, *Understanding Cooperatives: How to State a Cooperative.* rd.usda.gov/files /CIR45-14.pdf

Cooperative Development Institute, *Co-op 101: A Guide to Starting a Cooperative.* uwcc.wisc.edu/pdf/guide%20to%20starting%20a%20 cooperative.pdf

BC Co-op Association provides resources for forming and running co-ops. bcca.coop/

Co-op Law.org, *Choice of Entity.* co-oplaw.org/governance-operations /entity/

The People's Law Library of Maryland, *Basics of Forming and Maintaining Cooperatives in Maryland.* peoples-law.org/basics-forming-and -maintaining-cooperatives-maryland

For-Benefit Corporations

Corporate Laws Committee, American Bar Association Business Law Section, *Benefit Corporation White Paper.* jstor.org/stable/23526794 ?seq=1#page_scan_tab_contents

Benefit Corporation, *State by State Status of Legislation.* benefitcorp.net /policymakers/state-by-state-status

Happiness Lessons
for the Workplace

Mahatma Gandhi said, "Be the change that you wish to see in the world." While being completely happy is not a requirement for working on issues of happiness policy, it is important to consider and care for one's own happiness. When making happiness the purpose of government, it is important to also consider the personal happiness of government workers at every level, including administrative staff and appointed and elected officials. This can be addressed in the workplace. Each workplace has its own unique circumstances, and happiness practices are not one size fits all. Finding the workplace happiness practices that will benefit people's happiness entails a willingness to experiment and an ability to adapt as information emerges. Because everyone is different, it is important that people have a choice and are never forced to develop or engage in personal happiness practices. Enforcing happiness skill development or habits, even when it is scientifically known to lead to happiness, can potentially lead to misery for the person who has no choice. In addition, special caution should be taken to ensure that a person's emotions, such as their happiness or positivity level, should never be used as an evaluation metric in employee performance, as this imparts a draconian element to happiness and can lead to faking happiness, misery and depression or anxiety.

It may be the function of the happiness officers to receive the training and education to raise awareness, share knowledge, and transmit skills for personal happiness, or to bring in the trained experts who provide this training and skill development to employees, or a combination of both.

In this appendix, core lessons from the field of positive psychology are covered, with ways to integrate mindfulness, gratitude, and giving practices in the workplace. The practices presented in this appendix are places to begin the process of enhancing the happiness of a workforce so that people working on happiness matters can be the change they wish to see. They can be used as a basis for learning how to impart knowledge and skills, and for understanding the subject areas for experts.

Mindfulness Practices for the Workplace

Mindfulness has been proven to reduce stress and increase physical health.[1] Reducing stress helps people to deal more effectively with difficult situations and to be more resourceful and resilient in the face of challenges.

Mindfulness can be defined as the ability to be fully present and to see things as they really are (instead of how one wishes them to be) with kindness and without judgment. Mindfulness is a happiness skill that can be developed through practice.[2] This is why the word "practice" is used in the term *mindfulness practice.*

Breath Meditation Practices

Breath meditation is simply taking a few moments to pay attention to the breath. Learning how to focus on the breath develops the capacity to stay in the present and eventually see things as they really are. The most important aspect of developing this skill is noticing how difficult it is to simply focus on the breath. Noticing the mind not focusing on the breath, but being carried away by thoughts, worries, feelings, judgments, or other distractions, and bringing it back to focusing on the breath is the practice of developing the skill of mindfulness.

Breath meditation practice can be used at the beginning of meetings. Before starting this practice, give meeting participants an explanation about how to practice mindfulness. Ask people to put away cell phones or other distractions. Begin by taking thirty seconds to sit in silence and focus on the breath at the commencement of a meeting. Over time, build up to one or two minutes before beginning the meeting. If done regularly, meetings will be more productive and people will come to look forward to the few moments of silence.

Loving Kindness Practices

Loving kindness practice develops a person's capacity for positivity.[3] It is also thought to expand the capacity for compassion and wisdom. Compassion can be defined as the ability to see when others are hurting and take helpful action. Wisdom can be defined as the ability to know whether actions will be helpful or harmful. Loving kindness practice can be used to help solve difficult problems or for projects or processes that present challenges. It can be practiced by an individual, or by a team as part of a way to resolve conflict and find solutions. A caveat to loving kindness practice is that it should not be used instead of conflict resolution or other interventions when there are problems. It should be used in addition to interventions for problem solving, as a support for such interventions. Over time, loving kindness practice develops one's capacity for positivity, compassion, and wisdom.

Loving kindness practices entail using a series of phrases directed towards a person, followed by a short time to notice the thoughts, feelings, and impulses that arise after stating the phrases for that person. Loving kindness practice phrases are usually repeated silently, in two or more rounds. The phrases start first for oneself, then for someone one dearly loves, then for a family member, then a friend, then someone one does not know well (such as a grocery clerk or bank teller), then someone one does not like, concluding with the phrases repeated but for all people, then repeating the round. The phrases are: May I be happy, may I be healthy, may I be at ease, followed by a pause to notice the thoughts that arise, then: May (name of a person one loves) be happy, then repeat the phrases for a family member, a friend, someone you do not know, someone you do not like, until the last set in the round: may all people be happy, may all people be healthy, may all people be at ease.

Gratitude Practices

Habitually expressing gratitude is shown to increase happiness and satisfaction with life.[4] Gratitude also increases the appreciated person's sense of happiness and well-being. Gratitude practices entail expressive gratitude practices and reflective gratitude practices. Expressive gratitude practices involve expressing gratitude to another person. Reflective gratitude practice involves contemplation.

Expressive Gratitude Practices for the Workplace

Expressive gratitude practices entail expressing gratitude to another person. Practicing gratitude in this way can increase the happiness of both the person expressing the gratitude and the person who is being appreciated. It is important that the expression of gratitude is genuine and appropriate. Developing reflective gratitude skills can help establish a basis for genuine gratitude for other people. The simplest form of expressive gratitude practice is to say *thank you*, while expressing the reason for gratitude. This is an important and often overlooked gratitude skill. Gratitude skills can also be developed by regularly sending written notes in a card or email that contains only the expression of gratitude. When introducing these two gratitude practices into the workplace, it is best if the person in a position of authority use these practices with their employees and colleagues for a few months to a year, before inviting workers in the workplace to develop their own expressive gratitude skills.

Reflective Gratitude Practices for the Workplace

Reflective gratitude practices entails contemplation. Developing reflective gratitude skills can increase a person's happiness as well as interpersonal skills.[5] Keeping a gratitude journal is one reflective gratitude practice. Gratitude journals are similar to daily diaries but one writes about the thing or things for which one is grateful. These can be material things, people, events, or anything else. Another reflective gratitude practice is to contemplate three things that went well in one's day and identify at least one reason why each thing went well. This can be done as an entry into a gratitude journal or as a silent contemplation. A third reflective practice that can be done in the workplace with others is to identify all of the things that went well over the course of a specific time or project and discuss why they went well. This gratitude practice can be incorporated into a team meeting or as part of a strategy session.

Generosity Practices

Generosity increases the happiness of the person giving.[6] Generosity is often expressed with gifts of material objects or money, which are often not appropriate in the workplace. Office-place generosity can be practiced by giving time and full attention to a colleague or employee. Time can be given as part of the work process, or by taking lunch or a break with another person. Offering to help someone finish a task, helping someone get the resources they need to do their work, or finding ways to make someone's task easier can be ways to express generosity. Giving advice when it is asked for can also be an expression of generosity. Mentoring someone or helping someone network is also a way to express generosity.

Another example of an office practice for generosity is office sack lunches, where employees bring their lunch from home or the office provides lunch to everyone. Anyone at the office can participate. An additional opportunity for a generosity practice during sack lunches is when an employee gives a short presentation on a fun and amusing topic during lunch, such as how to kite sail, photograph wild animals, or the highlights of a favorite sports game. A sign-up board may be kept in a break room or online whereby anyone can sign up to present. It is helpful if some guidelines are given for the topics to present, to ensure that presentations are not offensive, incite gossip, or go on too long. The guidelines should also include a short explanation that giving one's full attention to someone while they present is a generosity practice. This can give everyone the opportunity to give their time and attention to each other during lunch and for the presentation.

There are many small things a person can do in the workplace to practice generosity. As people practice generosity, more ways to practice occur to them.

When practicing generosity at work, two factors that are important to account for are reciprocity and fairness. Generosity should not be practiced with an expectation of getting something back or as a way to give something back. It should not be a reward or an incentive. Generosity does not involve an exchange. Expecting something back when giving does not yield the happiness benefits of pure generosity. However, once recipients of generosity have been on the receiving end, they should have the opportunity to express gratitude or make some small gesture of reciprocity before benefiting from further generosity. This is because generosity over-expressed without reciprocity can lead to resentment instead of happiness on the part of the people who give and receive.

When practicing generosity in the workplace it is important not to give in a way that generates an atmosphere of favoritism or unfairness. This can come about unintentionally because it is natural for people to want to help other people who are most like them. If an office leader or supervisor occasionally takes an employee for a working or non-working lunch, then all of their employees should be invited to lunch occasionally as well, so that no one feels left out. Similarly, if an office leader or supervisor mentors someone, then all employees should have access to mentors who can give similar help.

Strategy Resources

There is a plethora of resources to help community organizers form a strategy to influence policymakers. In this appendix, three are outlined. The Community Tool Box[1] is a website that provides a wide array of resources from the basics of understanding what is meant by policy to how to sustain a policy change once it has been implemented. The website includes checklists for each chapter, examples of successful campaigns and, where appropriate, PowerPoint presentations. It also provides links to other online resources for community change makers. There are tools and resources for developing, planning, implementing, using media, and monitoring and evaluating policy changes. For example, Chapter 25: Implementing Promising Community Interventions gives practice steps for giving input to the decision makers before a policy is adopted and includes tactics for changing policies already in place. Section one in Chapter 25 identifies eight sequential steps for changing policy. They are synthesized here as:

1. Planning, using a participatory strategic planning process.
2. Preparation, including doing all the necessary research and becoming expert on existing policies.
3. Personal contact with policymakers, other change agents, and anyone else you have to deal with.
4. Pulse of the community, knowing what the community's attitudes are, what citizens will accept, where to start in order to be successful.
5. Positivism, framing policy changes and their outcomes in a positive light.
6. Participation, including everyone affected by or concerned with the issue in planning and implementing policy change.
7. Publicity for your effort in general and for your suggested policy changes—and the reasons for them—in particular.
8. Persistence, monitoring and evaluating your actions, and keeping at it for as long as necessary.

The book *Troublemaker's Teaparty: A Manual for Effective Citizen Action*[2] by Charles Dobson is a practical resource for groups with limited resources. It directly addresses the tough issues of working with groups and organizations to make change. It gives readers practical guidance on bringing people together, gathering support, forming strategies, fundraising, and volunteer management. It also includes guidelines for managing conflict and for working cooperatively. In addition, it includes tips for troubleshooting, such as when a policymaker is unresponsive or unhelpful.

Nick Licata's book *Becoming a Citizen Activist: Stories, Strategies & Advice for Changing Our World*[3] gives practical actions for short or long term activism and individual or collective action. It contains practice steps with precautions for persuading policymakers to enact change. It also contains the foundations of media campaigns and an action plan for forming a citizen commission.

The Happiness Proclamation

Policymakers from presidents to mayors and city managers have used the Model Happiness Proclamation. The Model Happiness Proclamation can be used in whole or part.

Happiness Proclamation of
[Name here of region, office, or organization]

WHEREAS, the United Nations resolution 69/305, adopted July 19, 2011, "Happiness: towards a holistic approach to development" recognizes "that the Gross Domestic Product indicator by nature was not designed to and does not adequately reflect the happiness and well-being of people in a country" and encourages "additional measures that better capture the importance of the pursuit of happiness and well-being";

WHEREAS, _____ understands that "...the welfare of a nation can scarcely be inferred from a measure of national income," as stated by Simon Kuznets, who created the standard that became Gross Domestic Product;

WHEREAS, _____ understands that the terms "happiness and well-being" encompass many aspects of life, including but not limited to how people are feeling, people's satisfaction with their lives, and people's level of flourishing, as well as dimensions of the conditions of life in the areas of the economy, standard of living, work, time balance, government, environment, mental and physical health, community, social support, culture, education and lifelong learning, housing, transportation, information technology, and other dimensions of life;

WHEREAS, _____ acknowledges our role and responsibility for the happiness, well-being, quality of life, resilience and sustainability of our nation;

WHEREAS, _____ understands that the role of government is not to dictate actions by people or entities but to set the stage to ensure equal opportunities for people to pursue their own definition of happiness (within the limits of the law);

WHEREAS, _____ understands that measuring people's happiness and well-being is a way to gather important data that points the way for a just, healthy and resilient society, economy and environment;

WHEREAS, _____ understands the importance of creating a broad assessment of the happiness and well-being of its people, using both objective and subjective indicators of happiness and well-being, using the data to inform policy decisions, planning and program implementation;

NOW, THEREFORE, be it proclaimed that the _____ supports the concept of wider measures of happiness and well-being to guide public policy and allocation of resources.

_____ intends to explore available happiness and well-being subjective and objective metrics and data and the application of happiness and well-being metrics to guide public policy and allocation of resources.

_____ encourages people and organizations to participate in publicly available surveys and encourages efforts to conduct a random sampling of our population using surveys and ensuring surveys results are representative of the population.

_____ encourages conversations to revitalize and reframe the debate about what really matters in life and provoke richer broader debate on a local and national level about the use of subjective and objective metrics and data.

_____ will consider the issues and ideas raised through conversations and debates in its exploration of happiness and well-being subjective and objective metrics and data.

Signed on this day _____ at_____
(Signatures in this space)

Model Press Release for a Happiness Proclamation and for Announcing the Use of the Happiness Index

These model press releases are provided for adoption and adaptation. They can be used in whole or part.

Model Press Release for a Happiness Proclamation

FOR IMMEDIATE RELEASE: Day, Month, Numerical Day, Year
(PROJECT NAME) ISSUES A HAPPINESS PROCLAMATION
CONTACTS
Name, Title, Organization, Phone, Email

YOUR NATION, STATE, CITY, OR TOWN NAME—Is happiness the purpose of government? (Governmental body name here) thinks so. It has just made a happiness proclamation (Name of proclamation here).

Need Statement: Use a quote from a high-level official here about the need for the project. Note about quotes: An efficient way to get quotes is to interview the candidate, then derive a quote from the interview that they then can edit. A quote can be as short as *"The happiness of the people of (name of country, state, or area) is important and should be the focus of government."*

Project Description: Use this section to educate the public and media. In this section first clarify how happiness is being defined and second clearly state that the role of government is to secure the conditions for people to pursue happiness as they define it, and never to force people into behaviors or actions. Use a quote from an official or person working in a department or on a team.

Such as: "We're thrilled to take the lead in this exciting project," adds (Name of Official). "We understand our role as setting the conditions for happiness, because everybody defines happiness in their own unique way. There is enough happiness and well-being science that we can now align policies to securing people's opportunities for the pursuit of happiness; which is what we see as the purpose of government. We have great hope that our work will lead to positive action for greater happiness, social justice, and both economic and environmental health."

The (name of agency, office, or other organization) defines happiness widely to encompass circumstances of life that include community, economy, education, environment, government, health, lifelong learning and culture, psychological well-being, social support, time balance, and work.

Motivation Quote. Use a quote from a community member. An sample motivation quote: "We are excited to support this initiative to bring quality of life to the forefront," says (name), (title). "It's wonderful that (name of country or area) is joining other countries around the world in this movement. We believe that our area will take a leadership position with demonstrable policies and programs that enhance our area's happiness and well-being."

Supporting Quote: This quote shows support from an important policymaker in a supporting role to the officials and office issuing the proclamation. It should be from someone highly respected and well-known by the public. An sample supporting quote: "A Happiness Proclamation is an important first step towards promoting the happiness of everyone in our region," adds (name of supporting person). "This is a vitally important endeavor."

Action: To learn more and get involved with (project name) email (email address), sign up for timely updates and information on Twitter, (twitter account) or sign up for our newsletter at (newsletter sign up link).

Learn more: Website Link and BOILERPLATE HERE about agency or organization.

Model Press Release for a Announcing the Use of the Happiness Index

FOR IMMEDIATE RELEASE: Day, Month, Numerical Day, Year

(PROJECT NAME) LAUNCHES A HAPPINESS INDEX
CONTACTS
Name, Title, Organization, Phone, Email

YOUR NATION, STATE, CITY, OR TOWN NAME —Can you measure *happiness?* (your project name) thinks so. In association with (list project partners), it is releasing the first comprehensive survey of happiness in this region, as part of the (name of your project).

Need Statement: Use a quote from a leader here about the need for the project. Here is the quote we used. (Note about quotes: The most efficient way to get quotes is to interview the candidate, then derive a quote from the interview that they then can edit. You are less likely to get the quote you need if you simply ask for a quote stating the need, etc.)

"You get what you measure," says (official name). "For too long we've measured the wrong things—Gross Domestic Product doesn't tell us whether we have a good quality of life or a sustainable society. The Happiness Index, which includes income and other economic measures, but goes beyond it, is a good way to start measuring the important things we care about, so we can actually achieve them."

Project Description: Use a quote from your project lead or another person on your team.

"We're thrilled to take the lead in this exciting project," adds (project lead). "We hope this effort leads to positive action for greater happiness, social justice, and both economic and environmental health."

The Happiness Index is now online at (your website). Anyone may take the survey and receive an immediate evaluation of personal well-being for each of the domains of happiness identified by international researchers: *community, culture, health, economy, environment, government, lifelong learning, psychological well-being, satisfaction with life, social support, time balance, and work.*

The survey takes a holistic approach to well-being and asks poignant questions that allow reflection and insight.

Motivation Quote: *You can use this one from the Happiness Alliance, ask for another, or supply your own from another source.*

"It takes about 12 minutes to complete," says Laura Musikanski, Executive Director of the Happiness Alliance. "But you'll find it's worth the time because it really makes you think about your life and how to improve it. It's part of a global movement to add quality of life and sustainability to our assessments of progress. The results will be useful to individuals, organizations, and policymakers who want to base their efforts to increase well-being on solid science and comprehensive information."

Supporting Quote: This quote shows support from important organizations that are members of the team.

"The survey is critical for all of our actions to promote happiness and compassion for everyone in our region," adds (name) of (name of an organization). "We are delighted to support this vitally important project."

To learn more and get involved with (project name) email (email address), sign up for timely updates and information on Twitter, (twitter account) or sign up for our newsletter at (newsletter sign up link).

And take the survey now at: Your Website

BOILERPLATE HERE about your organization.

Model Happiness Minister or Officer Job Description

The Model Happiness Minister or Official job description lays out a list of responsibilities that describe the tasks entailed to integrate happiness into government. This list can be adopted in whole, in part, or used as a starting place to set responsibilities for unique circumstances.

The tasks are:

+ Work with top level officials to issue a happiness proclamation followed by a happiness resolution stating intent, goals, and methods.
+ Educate and inform government leaders about the role of happiness in government through various methods, from training sessions, online modules, and informative presentations to conferences and summits, as well as modules and methods for civil servants in each department to understand how to use happiness and well-being to guide policy.
+ Educate the general population about the relevance of happiness to governmental process and policy, and the impacts on individuals, ensuring a nation's people that the government's role is not to prescribe or force actions for personal happiness, but to secure the conditions for personal choices and actions for happiness.
+ Educate the private sector and community-based organizations and work with both towards cooperation and development of a happy and sustainable area with high quality of life for all.
+ Reach out to the international community to create pathways for learning, sharing, and communication between governments, NGOs, and the private sector.
+ Work with governmental functions that provide services to the public to find ways to improve the happiness and well-being of those served through such means as process reformation, intergovernmental function cooperation, goal setting, and exit surveys for people served; and work

with high-level officials across departments providing services to the public to facilitate cooperation and process reformation that increases public happiness, well-being, quality of life, resilience, thriving, and sustainability.

- Conduct annual measurements of the happiness and well-being of a nation, region, city, town, or community using survey-based and objective indicator instruments, analyze the data, and provide reports to each department and the public with trends, policy and program recommendations, and recommendations for individual actions for happiness.
- Develop policy and program happiness screening tools for the government overall and for each department and work with each department to implement and use them, as well as provide quarterly and annual reporting on policy and program outcomes, including the screening process, and if a policy or program is passed, reporting on the outcomes and impacts on happiness.

Social Media Guide

Social media is an important platform for engaging the community. It is used by a growing number of policymakers in a growing number of ways, from raising awareness to gathering feedback to garnering support. This appendix explains four aspects of using social media: purpose, content, profile, and audience.

Purpose

It is important to have a clear purpose before using social media. Policymakers have used social media for the purposes of delivering news, educating the public, building support, and gathering feedback.

Social media is widely considered a good platform for broadcasting information to a wide audience. Sometimes it is used as the first channel for announcements and other news, thereby rewarding social media audiences, which in turn drives up the number of followers, friends, views, or likes. Social media platforms have been used by policymakers to announce intent, such as a decision to measure the happiness of a population. They have also been used to invite people to an event, such as a press release or town meeting.

Social media platforms are also useful tools for educating and empowering the public. Best practices are to consistently provide content that is of value to the audience in small "bite-sized" formats. For example, a program to install bike lanes in a city or community might entail regular posts about aspects of bicycle riding safety, maps of where bike lanes are in a city, information about a bicycling event, and pictures of a high-level policymaker biking to work, etc.

Social media can also be used to build support. Social media platforms have different nomenclature for their audiences: followers, contacts, friends, connections, etc. The most common way to demonstrate support is by the size of your audience. Another is the number of likes, hearts, thumbs up, or other icons showing a reaction. A third way is the number of times content is shared or reposted. Some social media platforms allow for comments and the number and quality of comments can also demonstrate support from an audience, but can also demonstrate the opposite. If comments are allowed, it is important to manage them as this feature can be vulnerable to inappropriate spam. For some media platforms, the number of times a link is clicked on cannot be used to demonstrate support as the number of clicks is not recorded, thus posts with links should often not be included when measuring demonstration of support.

Social media can also be used to gather information from an audience. This is a popular use at events or for time-bound situations. In such cases social media platforms with smaller content requirements, such as Twitter, Instagram, Snapchat, or other platforms are used. When a larger amount of information or feedback is desired or anonymity will encourage more participation, a website portal or e-form can be a good option.

Content

Content is the term used for anything that is placed on social media. Content can be written work, a photo, an infographic, or links. Often content delivered on one social media site is repurposed from one to another platform. For example, a photo posted on Instagram can also be posted in Twitter with a short caption or link, and also to LinkedIn or Facebook with a longer explanation. Another option is to repost or share content from one social media site to other sites. In this case, the content is reposted without additional information.

On social media sites, the competition for attention is high. In addition to posting high quality and visually stimulating content, it is possible to promote content by paying to increase the number of times an audience will see it or for an audience that is not already a follower, friend, or contact to see it. Paying for content to be displayed is called "boosting." Boosting should only be done when content will be of value to the audience, or it can backfire and cause an audience to shrink or ignore future content.

Profile

When using social media, a choice of profile must be made. Depending on the medium, the choice may be between a personal account or an organization, public figure, or cause account. Personal accounts are set up by an individual and managed by that individual. The other kind of accounts may be managed by representatives.

When setting up a Twitter account, a unique name is required, which begins with the @ sign and is limited to fifteen characters. To create an account, an email address is needed. Only one email can be associated with an account, so it is important not to use the same email for a personal and professional or organizational accounts. The account can then be designated as a personal account or an organizational account, or converted to an organizational account from a personal one at any time. (A caveat to changing types of accounts: the email associated with an account that is converted from personal to organizational cannot be used to create another personal account.) Tweets can include texts, links, and photos.

Instagram allows for organizational accounts, which it calls business accounts. The first step is to create an account and convert it to a business account in the account settings with the "switch to business profile" option. Information about the organization is filled in by going first to the "edit profile" function and then to the "business contact information" setting. An Instagram account can be linked to a Facebook page, and content posted to Instagram will automatically post to the linked Facebook page.

LinkedIn pages for an organization can be created with the company page option. Originally LinkedIn was used for finding employment and offering job opportunities, but more and more it is used for information sharing. Information can be added by the person who creates the LinkedIn page. The person who creates the LinkedIn page is the administrator and can add other administrators. Employees or other stakeholders with LinkedIn accounts can become members, and anyone can "follow" an organization's LinkedIn page. An organization can create Showcase pages as part of its LinkedIn page to focus on specific topics or issues.

YouTube accounts, called "channels," require a two-step process. First an account must be created, then a channel must be created. Channels are where videos are posted. Accounts are automatically created by linking to a Gmail account but can be created with a company or personal email address via the "create account" function. To create an account and a channel without a Gmail account, it is necessary to include a telephone number for text or telephone call for verification for both the account and the channel (two separate verification processes are necessary). Once a YouTube account is created, a "creator studio" is attached to the account. In the creator studio, a channel can be created. Once a YouTube channel is created, the account name can be replaced with the organizational name through the "use your business name or other name" option in the first step of setting up a channel. Information about the organization can be added by the "customize channel" function within the creator studio. A caveat to YouTube accounts: changing names can result in the loss of all videos and analytics.

Facebook accounts for individual people are called profiles and for organizations are called pages. Profiles can have friends and pages can be liked. Individual profiles are limited to 5,000 friends, and can be converted into pages, whereby a page can be liked, but the friend option is not available. To create a page, an individual logs onto their profile account, creates the page, and thereby is an administrator of that page. Other people with Facebook profiles can be designated administrators. Administrators can choose what information is listed in the "about" section of the Facebook page, so that it reflects the organization and not the personal information of administrators. It is also possible to create Facebook groups, which are discussion forums, and events, which are timebound. It is possible to manage all of the content posted on a page so that only administrators can post content. It is not possible to turn off comments to posts, but it is possible to hide or delete individual comments, or block profane words. When content is posted to a page, it also appears on the homepages of the profiles who liked the page. Facebook changes options and requirements over time, so it is good to keep updated on their procedures.

Audience

On social media platforms, the size of the audience is considered important. The size of an audience can bring more attention to the content posted, and convey a greater level of respect to the organization's profile on the social media platform. Social media platforms have different names and functions for audiences.

Twitter has followers. Following is one way to increase the number of followers. When following others you can follow people who follow similar profiles or organizations to you or yours. The number of followers can also be increased by following people who follow you. Posting high-quality content that followers retweet can also increase the number of followers. Commenting, hearting (instead of liking, a heart emoticon denotes approval), and retweeting followers' tweets can increase the attention followers give, and draw in more followers. Boosting can also increase the number of followers. Instagram also has followers. LinkedIn has connections for individuals and followers for organizations. Facebook has friends for individual profiles and likes for organizational pages. Similar tactics to Twitter can be used to increase audience on other social media platforms.

Questions and Answers
for Happiness Survey Takers

The text in this appendix can be used in whole or part and changed or adapted. It is based on feedback from years of use of the Happiness Index, and oriented to people who are using the Happiness Alliance's Happiness Index platform for gathering data, and partnering with the Happiness Alliance to provide tools and resources for developing personal happiness skills. If another platform is used, the language will need to be modified.

What is the Happiness Index and what does it measure?
The Happiness Index is a scientific measurement of happiness and well-being. It is a survey composed of questions about your life and the circumstances of your life. The circumstances of your life include your community, work, time-balance, health, and other aspects of life. We use a survey to measure your happiness because science and common sense tell us that the best way to understand how well you feel your life is going is to ask.

How do I know I can trust the survey? Won't my data be traced back to me?
When you take the Happiness Index, your data is protected under the European Union's Protection of Personal Data Directive 2016/679, regardless of the nation in which you take it. In simple terms, all of your answers to the questions in the Happiness Index will be kept anonymous, and information identifying you personally (your name, email, or ISP address) will never be shared, sold, or used for any purpose you do not agree to.

We are partnering with the Happiness Alliance, a nonprofit that has worked with cities, countries, communities, campuses, and companies worldwide. The Happiness Alliance is administering the survey and will provide us the data, ensuring your personal identification is protected.

Why should I taken the Happiness Index? What's in it for me?
When you take the Happiness Index, you directly contribute to the happiness movement, and a paradigm shift in our communities, society, and hearts whereby we put our happiness, each other's well-being, and the sustainability of our planet and future generations first. You also get your own self-assessment of your well-being, and can see how you score in relation to everybody else who has taken the survey. You can use the survey and your scores to contemplate your own happiness and how you think about happiness. You can also use it to engage in conversations at home, in your community, and at work about happiness and the purpose of life, work, and government.

Is there a baseline for happiness?
When you take the Happiness Index, you will get a score for your happiness in the various domains of happiness. These are: community, environment, government, health, lifelong learning and culture, satisfaction with life and affect (feelings), social support, standard of living, time balance, and work. A low score in a domain does not necessarily mean that you are unhappy, but it could mean that your life is out of balance. Over time, imbalance can lead to unhappiness. You will also see how you compare to others who have taken the survey. If your scores are lower than others, then you might want to reflect on what that means to you, and whether changes would bring you happiness. You can also find resources for how to develop your skills for being happy on the Happiness Alliance's website at happycounts.org.

The Happiness Index Questions

The methodology and source for each question in the Happiness Index has been published and is available for download on the Happiness Alliance webpage for researchers (happycounts.org/for-researchers). The questions are listed below.

Satisfaction with Life and Affect (Feelings)

Please imagine a ladder with steps numbered from zero at the bottom to ten at the top. Suppose we say that the top of the ladder represents the best possible life for you and the bottom of the ladder represents the worst possible. If the top step is 10 and the bottom step is 0, on which step of the ladder do you feel you personally stand at the present time?

Overall, how satisfied are you with your life nowadays?

Overall, to what extent do you feel the things you do in your life are worthwhile?

Overall, how happy did you feel yesterday?

Overall, how anxious did you feel yesterday?

Psychological Well-Being

To what extent do you agree with the following statements:

+ I lead a purposeful and meaningful life.
+ I am engaged and interested in my daily activities.
+ I am optimistic about my future.
+ Most days I feel a sense of accomplishment from what I do.
+ In general, I feel very positive about myself.

Health

In general, I would say my health is (poor, fair, good, very good, excellent).

Please indicate, how much of the time during the past week you had a lot of energy.

Please rate your level of satisfaction:
+ How satisfied were you with your ability to perform your daily living activities?
+ How satisfied were you with the quality of your exercise?

Time Balance

In a typical week, how much of your time are you able to spend doing the kinds of things that you enjoy?

Here are some statements about how things are going in your life. When indicating your agreement with each statement, please think specifically about how things were for you over the past week.
+ My life has been too rushed.
+ I have had plenty of spare time.

Community

How would you describe your feeling of belonging to your local community?

Please tell us how many of the following people you trust:
+ Your neighbors.
+ Businesses in your community.

Imagine that you lost a wallet or purse that contained two hundred dollars. Please indicate how likely you think it would be to have all of your money returned to you if it was found by someone who lives close by.

How satisfied are you with your personal safety in your city or town?

Using the scale below, please indicate how frequently you have done these activities in the past 12 months:
+ Volunteered your time to an organization.
+ Donated money to a charity.

Social Support

How satisfied are you with your personal relationships?

To what extent do you agree with the following statement:
+ People in my life care about me.

Please indicate how much of the time during the past week...
+ You felt loved.
+ You felt lonely.

Lifelong Learning, Arts and Culture

In your neighborhood or community, how satisfied you are with...

+ Your access to sports and recreational activities?
+ Your access to artistic and cultural activities?
+ Your access to activities to develop skills through informal education?

How often do you feel uncomfortable or out of place in your neighborhood because of your ethnicity, culture, race, skin color, language, accent, gender, sexual orientation, or religion?

Environment

How healthy is your physical environment?

How satisfied are you with the efforts being made to preserve the natural environment in your neighborhood?

How satisfied are you with the opportunities that you have to enjoy nature?

How satisfied are you with the air quality in your environment?

Government

State your level of agreement with the following statements:

+ Corruption is widespread throughout the government in my city or town.
+ The public officials in my city or town pay attention to what people think.

Please indicate how much confidence you have in the following organizations:

+ National government.
+ Local government.

Standard of Living / Economy

In general, how much stress do you feel about your personal finances?

How frequently do you find yourself just getting by financially and living paycheck to paycheck?

Please indicate how frequently you have had the following experience in the past 12 months:

+ You ate less because there wasn't enough food or money for food.

To what extent do you agree with the following statement:

+ I have enough money to buy things I want.

Work

Please answer the following questions about your satisfaction with your current working situation.

All things considered, how satisfied are you with your current work life? (Note: if you work or volunteer at more than one job, you should answer about the job you spend the longest time working at.)

How satisfied are you with the balance between the time you spend on your job and the time you spend on other aspects of your life?

How much of the time do you find your current work life interesting?

Please state your level of agreement with each of these statements:

- Considering all my efforts and achievements in my job I feel I get paid appropriately.
- The conditions of my job allow me to be about as productive as I could be.
- I am allowed to decide how to go about getting my job done.

The Happiness Policy Screening Tool

The Happiness Policy Screening Tool is provided for adoption and adaptation. It can be used as a starting place for creating a unique screening tool or in whole without changing it.

■ Satisfaction with Life (SWL)

SWL 1. Satisfaction with life.

Will decrease satisfaction with life.	Unknown impact on satisfaction with life.	Neutral impact on satisfaction with life.	Will increase satisfaction with life.
1	2	3	4

SWL 2. Sense people have that things they do in their life are worthwhile.

Will decrease sense that things people do in their life are worthwhile.	Unknown impact on sense that things people do in their life are worthwhile.	Neutral impact on sense that things people do in their life are worthwhile.	Will increase sense that things people do in their life are worthwhile.
1	2	3	4

SWL 3. Sense of happiness.

Will decrease sense of happiness.	Unknown impact on sense of happiness.	Neutral impact on sense of happiness.	Will increase sense of happiness.
1	2	3	4

SWL 4. Sense of anxiety.

Will increase sense of anxiety.	Unknown impact on sense of anxiety.	Neutral impact on sense of anxiety.	Will decrease sense of anxiety.
1	2	3	4

■ Psychological Well-Being (PWB)

PWB 1. Sense of leading a purposeful and meaningful life.

Will decrease sense of leading a purposeful and meaningful life.	Unknown impact on sense of leading a purposeful and meaningful life.	Neutral impact on sense of leading a purposeful and meaningful life.	Will increase sense of leading a purposeful and meaningful life.
1	2	3	4

PWB 2. Sense of engagement and interest in daily activities.

Will decrease sense of engagement and interest in daily activities.	Unknown impact on sense of engagement and interest in daily activities.	Neutral impact on sense of engagement and interest in daily activities.	Will increase sense of engagement and interest in daily activities.
1	2	3	4

PWB 3. Sense of optimism about the future.

Will decrease sense of optimism about the future.	Unknown impact on sense of optimism about the future.	Neutral impact on sense of optimism about the future.	Will increase sense of optimism about the future.
1	2	3	4

PWB 4. Sense of accomplishment that people have from what they do.

Will decrease sense of accomplishment.	Unknown impact on sense of accomplishment.	Neutral impact on sense of accomplishment.	Will increase sense of accomplishment.
1	2	3	4

PWB 5. Sense of feeling positive about oneself.

Will decrease sense of feeling positive about oneself.	Unknown impact on sense of feeling positive about oneself.	Neutral impact on sense of feeling positive about oneself.	Will increase sense of feeling positive about oneself.
1	2	3	4

PWB 6. Access to mental health care.

Will decrease access to mental health care.	Unknown impact on access to mental health care.	Neutral impact on access to mental health care.	Will increase access to mental health care.
1	2	3	4

■ Health (H)

H 1. Sense of being physically healthy.

Will decrease sense of being physically healthy.	Unknown impact on sense of being physically healthy.	Neutral impact on sense of being physically healthy.	Will increase sense of being physically healthy.
1	2	3	4

H 2. Healthy life expectancy.

Will decrease healthy life expectancy.	Unknown impact on healthy life expectancy.	Neutral impact on healthy life expectancy.	Will increase healthy life expectancy.
1	2	3	4

H 3. Sense of having a lot of energy.

Will decrease sense of having a lot of energy.	Unknown impact on sense of having a lot of energy.	Neutral impact on sense of having a lot of energy.	Will increase sense of having a lot of energy.
1	2	3	4

H 4. Percent of population with health coverage.

Will decrease percentage of population with health coverage.	Unknown impact on percentage of population with health coverage.	Neutral impact on percentage of population with health coverage.	Will increase percentage of population with health coverage.
1	2	3	4

H 5. Satisfaction with ability to perform daily living activities.

Will decrease satisfaction with ability to perform daily living activities.	Unknown impact on satisfaction with ability to perform daily living activities.	Neutral impact on satisfaction with ability to perform daily living activities.	Will increase satisfaction with ability to perform daily living activities.
1	2	3	4

H 6. Satisfaction with quality of exercise.

Will decrease satisfaction with quality of exercise.	Unknown impact on satisfaction with quality of exercise.	Neutral impact on satisfaction with quality of exercise.	Will increase satisfaction with quality of exercise.
1	2	3	4

H 7. Walkability index for an area (e.g. US EPA's Walkability Index, Walkscore.com, etc.).

Will decrease walkability index in an area.	Unknown impact on walkability index in an area.	Neutral impact on walkability index in an area.	Will increase walkability index in an area.
1	2	3	4

■ Time Balance (TB)

TB 1. The amount of time people feel they are able to spend doing the kinds of things that they enjoy.

Will decrease the amount of time people feel they are able to spend doing the kinds of things that they enjoy.	Unknown impact on the amount of time people feel they are able to spend doing the kinds of things that they enjoy.	Neutral impact on the amount of time people feel they are able to spend doing the kinds of things that they enjoy.	Will increase the amount of time people feel they are able to spend doing the kinds of things that they enjoy.
1	2	3	4

TB 2. Leisure time spent with friends or family, or on hobbies or out of doors, away from home in previous 12 months.

Will decrease the amount of leisure time spent with friends or family, or on hobbies or out of doors.	Unknown impact on amount of leisure time spent with friends or family, or on hobbies or out of doors.	Neutral impact on amount of leisure time spent with friends or family, or on hobbies or out of doors.	Will increase the amount of leisure time spent with friends or family, or on hobbies or out of doors.
1	2	3	4

TB 3. Sense that life has been too rushed.

Will increase sense that life has been too rushed.	Unknown impact on sense that life has been too rushed.	Neutral impact on sense that life has been too rushed.	Will decrease sense that life has been too rushed.
1	2	3	4

TB 4. Proportion of people who are working very long hours (50 hours or more a week).

Will increase the proportion of people who are working very long hours.	Unknown impact on the proportion of people who are working very long hours.	Neutral impact on the proportion of people who are working very long hours.	Will decrease the proportion of people who are working very long hours.
1	2	3	4

TB 5. Sense of having plenty of spare time.

Will decrease sense of having plenty of spare time.	Unknown impact on sense of having plenty of spare time.	Neutral impact on sense of having plenty of spare time.	Will increase sense of having plenty of spare time.
1	2	3	4

TB 6. Time devoted to leisure and personal care (amount of minutes or hours per day that, on average, full-time employed people spend on leisure and personal care activities).

Will decrease time devoted to leisure and personal care.	Unknown impact on time devoted to leisure and personal care.	Neutral impact on time devoted to leisure and personal care.	Will increase time devoted to leisure and personal care.
1	2	3	4

■ Community (C)

C 1. Sense of belonging to a local community.

Will decrease sense of belonging to a local community.	Unknown impact on sense of belonging to a local community.	Neutral impact on sense of belonging to a local community.	Will increase sense of belonging to a local community.
1	2	3	4

C 2. Proportion of population that donates to a charity and frequency of donations.

Will decrease proportion of population that donates and frequency of donations.	Unknown impact on proportion of population that donates and frequency of donations.	Neutral impact on proportion of population that donates and frequency of donations.	Will increase proportion of population that donates and frequency of donations.
1	2	3	4

C 3. Proportion of population that volunteers time and frequency of time spent volunteering over a time period (informal and formal volunteering of time).

Will decrease proportion of population that volunteers and frequency of time spent volunteering.	Unknown impact on proportion of population that volunteers and frequency of time spent volunteering.	Neutral impact on proportion of population that volunteers and frequency of time spent volunteering.	Will increase proportion of population that volunteers and frequency of time spent volunteering.
1	2	3	4

C 4. Sense of trust in neighbors.

Will decrease sense of trust in neighbors.	Unknown impact on sense of trust in neighbors.	Neutral impact on sense of trust in neighbors.	Will increase sense of trust in neighbors.
1	2	3	4

C 5. Sense of trust in businesses in one's community.

Will decrease sense of trust in businesses in one's community.	Unknown impact on sense of trust in businesses in one's community.	Neutral impact on sense of trust in businesses in one's community.	Will increase sense of trust in businesses in one's community.
1	2	3	4

C 6. Satisfaction with personal safety.

Will decrease satisfaction with personal safety.	Unknown impact on satisfaction with personal safety.	Neutral impact on satisfaction with personal safety.	Will increase satisfaction with personal safety.
1	2	3	4

C 7. Domestic violence (against women, children, or men).

Will increase domestic violence.	Unknown impact on domestic violence.	Neutral impact on domestic violence.	Will decrease domestic violence.
1	2	3	4

C 8. Violent crime rates in an area.

Will increase violent crime rates.	Unknown impact on violent crime rates.	Neutral impact on violent crime rates.	Will decrease violent crime rates.
1	2	3	4

■ Social Support (S)

S 1. Satisfaction with personal relationships.

Will decrease satisfaction with personal relationships.	Unknown impact on satisfaction with personal relationships.	Neutral impact on satisfaction with personal relationships	Will increase satisfaction with personal relationships.
1	2	3	4

S 2. Percentage of children in primary school receiving happiness and well-being (skill development in such areas as mindfulness, gratitude, generosity, empathy, emotional intelligence, decision making, perseverance, active listening, creative thinking, etc.) education.

Will decrease percentage of children in primary school receiving happiness and well-being education.	Unknown impact on percentage of children in primary school receiving happiness and well-being education.	Neutral impact on percentage of children in primary school receiving happiness and well-being education.	Will increase percentage of children in primary school receiving happiness and well-being education.
1	2	3	4

S 3. Sense that people have that someone in their life cares about them.

Will decrease sense that someone in their life cares about them.	Unknown impact on sense that someone in their life cares about them.	Neutral impact on sense that someone in their life cares about them.	Will increase sense that someone in their life cares about them.
1	2	3	4

S 4. Percentage of population covered by social protection programs (coverage for unemployment, health care, disability, work-place injury, old age, etc).

Will decrease percentage of population covered by social protection programs.	Unknown impact on percentage of population covered by social protection programs.	Neutral impact on percentage of population covered by social protection programs.	Will increase percentage of population covered by social protection programs.
1	2	3	4

S 5. Sense of feeling lonely.

Will increase sense of feeling lonely.	Unknown impact on sense of feeling lonely.	Neutral impact on sense of feeling lonely.	Will decrease sense of feeling lonely.
1	2	3	4

S 6. Proportion of persons with a severe mental disorder (psychosis, bipolar affective disorder, moderate-severe depression, substance abuse disorder, etc.) who are using mental health services.

Will decrease proportion of persons with a severe mental disorder who are using mental health services.	Unknown impact on proportion of persons with a severe mental disorder who are using mental health services.	Neutral impact on proportion of persons with a severe mental disorder who are using mental health services.	Will increase proportion of persons with a severe mental disorder who are using mental health services.
1	2	3	4

S 7. Sense of feeling loved.

Will decrease sense of feeling loved.	Unknown impact on sense of feeling loved.	Neutral impact on sense of feeling loved.	Will increase sense of feeling loved.
1	2	3	4

S 8. Met demand for family planning.

Will decrease met demand for family planning.	Unknown impact on met demand for family planning.	Neutral impact on met demand for family planning.	Will increase met demand for family planning.
1	2	3	4

■ Lifelong Learning, Arts and Culture (L)

L 1. Satisfaction with access to sports and recreational activities.

Will decrease satisfaction with access to sports and recreational activities.	Unknown impact on satisfaction with access to sports and recreational activities.	Neutral impact on satisfaction with access to sports and recreational activities.	Will increase satisfaction with access to sports and recreational activities.
1	2	3	4

L 2. Satisfaction with access to artistic and cultural activities.

Will decrease satisfaction with access to artistic and cultural activities.	Unknown impact on satisfaction with access to artistic and cultural activities.	Neutral impact on satisfaction with access to artistic and cultural activities.	Will increase satisfaction with access to artistic and cultural activities.
1	2	3	4

L 3. Creation of jobs and promotion of local culture and products through sustainable tourism.

Will decrease creation of jobs and promotion of local culture and products through sustainable tourism.	Unknown impact on creation of jobs and promotion of local culture and products through sustainable tourism.	Neutral impact on creation of jobs and promotion of local culture and products through sustainable tourism.	Will increase creation of jobs and promotion of local culture and products through sustainable tourism.
1	2	3	4

L 4. Satisfaction with educational systems or schools in one's city or area in which one lives.

Will decrease satisfaction with educational systems or schools in one's city or area in which one lives.	Unknown impact on satisfaction with educational systems or schools in one's city or area in which one lives.	Neutral impact on satisfaction with educational systems or schools in one's city or area in which one lives.	Will increase satisfaction with educational systems or schools in one's city or area in which one lives.
1	2	3	4

L 5. Satisfaction with access to develop skills through informal education.

Will decrease satisfaction with access to develop skills through informal education.	Unknown impact on satisfaction with access to develop skills through informal education.	Neutral impact on satisfaction with access to develop skills through informal education.	Will increase satisfaction with access to develop skills through informal education.
1	2	3	4

L 6. Adult literacy rates.

Will decrease adult literacy rates.	Unknown impact on adult literacy rates.	Neutral impact on adult literacy rates.	Will increase adult literacy rates.
1	2	3	4

L 7. Completion rates of upper secondary education (upper secondary education defined as high school education or education until 18–19 years of age).

Will decrease completion rates of upper secondary education.	Unknown impact on completion rates of upper secondary education.	Neutral impact on completion rates of upper secondary education.	Will increase completion rates of upper secondary education.
1	2	3	4

L 8. Tertiary enrollment rates for women and men (tertiary education defined as higher, advanced, or professional education).

Will decrease tertiary enrollment rates for women and men.	Unknown impact on tertiary enrollment rates for women and men.	Neutral impact on tertiary enrollment rates for women and men.	Will increase tertiary enrollment rates for women and men.
1	2	3	4

L 9. Sense of feeling uncomfortable or out of place because of ethnicity, culture, race, skin color, language, accent, gender, sexual orientation, or religion.

Will increase sense of feeling uncomfortable or out of place because of ethnicity, culture, race, skin color, language, accent, gender, sexual orientation, or religion.	Unknown impact on sense of feeling uncomfortable or out of place because of ethnicity, culture, race, skin color, language, accent, gender, sexual orientation, or religion.	Neutral impact on sense of feeling un-comfortable or out of place because of ethnicity, culture, race, skin color, language, accent, gender, sexual orientation, or religion.	Will decrease sense of feeling uncomfortable or out of place because of ethnicity, culture, race, skin color, language, accent, gender, sexual orientation, or religion.
1	2	3	4

L 10. Proportion of population that are victims of physical or sexual harassment proportionate to city or area population by sex, age, disability status, and place of occurrence, in the previous 12 months.

Will increase proportion of population that are victims of physical or sexual harassment proportionate to city or area population.	Unknown impact on proportion of population that are victims of physical or sexual harassment proportionate to city or area population.	Neutral impact on proportion of population that are victims of physical or sexual harassment proportionate to city or area population.	Will decrease proportion of population that are victims of physical or sexual harassment proportionate to city or area population.
1	2	3	4

■ Environment (E)

E 1. Sense of how healthy the physical environment is.

Will decrease sense of how healthy the physical environment is.	Unknown impact on sense of how healthy the physical environment is.	Neutral impact on sense of how healthy the physical environment is.	Will increase sense of how healthy the physical environment is.
1	2	3	4

E 2. Number of deaths and illnesses from hazardous chemicals and air, water, and soil pollution and contamination in a year for a region or area.

Will increase number of deaths and illnesses from hazardous chemicals and air, water, and soil pollution and contamination.	Unknown impact on number of deaths and illnesses from hazardous chemicals and air, water, and soil pollution and contamination.	Neutral impact on number of deaths and illnesses from hazardous chemicals and air, water, and soil pollution and contamination.	Will decrease number of deaths and illnesses from hazardous chemicals and air, water, and soil pollution and contamination.
1	2	3	4

E 3. Satisfaction with efforts being made to preserve the natural environment.

Will decrease satisfaction with efforts being made to preserve the natural environment.	Unknown impact on satisfaction with efforts being made to preserve the natural environment.	Neutral impact on satisfaction with efforts being made to preserve the natural environment.	Will increase satisfaction with efforts being made to preserve the natural environment.
1	2	3	4

E 4. Protected areas overlay with biodiversity in a region or area (i.e., protection of terrestrial and marine areas, protection of biodiversity areas, protection of zero extinction sites).

Will decrease amount of protected areas overlay with biodiversity.	Unknown impact on amount of protected areas overlay with biodiversity.	Neutral impact on amount of protected areas overlay with biodiversity.	Will increase amount of protected areas overlay with biodiversity.
1	2	3	4

E 5. Plant and animal species on International Union for Conservation of Nature (IUCN) Red List for a region or area.

Will increase number of plant and animal species on IUCN Red List.	Unknown impact on plant and animal species on IUCN Red List.	Neutral impact on plant and animal species on IUCN Red List.	Will decrease number of plant and animal species on IUCN Red List.
1	2	3	4

E 6. Satisfaction with opportunities to enjoy nature.

Will decrease satisfaction with opportunities to enjoy nature.	Unknown impact on satisfaction with opportunities to enjoy nature.	Neutral impact on satisfaction with opportunities to enjoy nature.	Will increase satisfaction with opportunities to enjoy nature.
1	2	3	4

E 7. Area of public and green space as a proportion of total town or city space.

Will decrease area of public and green space as a proportion of total city space.	Unknown impact on area of public and green space as a proportion of total city space.	Neutral impact on area of public and green space as a proportion of total city space.	Will increase area of public and green space as a proportion of total city space.
1	2	3	4

E 8. Satisfaction with air quality.

Will decrease satisfaction with air quality.	Unknown impact on satisfaction with air quality.	Neutral impact on satisfaction with air quality.	Will increase satisfaction with air quality.
1	2	3	4

E 9. Greenhouse gas emissions and other air pollutant emissions.

Will increase greenhouse gas emissions and other air pollutants.	Unknown impact on greenhouse gas emissions and other air pollutants.	Neutral impact on greenhouse gas emissions and other air pollutants.	Will decrease greenhouse gas emissions and other air pollutants.
1	2	3	4

■ Government (G)

G 1. Sense that corruption is widespread throughout the government.

Will increase sense that corruption is widespread throughout the government.	Unknown impact on sense that corruption is widespread throughout the government.	Neutral impact on sense that corruption is widespread throughout the government.	Will decrease sense that corruption is widespread throughout the government.
1	2	3	4

G 2. Corruption Perception Index (e.g. Transparency International scale, 0 is most corrupt, 100 is clean, or similar assessment).

Will increase Corruption Perception Index.	Unknown impact on Corruption Perception Index.	Neutral impact on Corruption Perception Index.	Will decrease Corruption Perception Index.
1	2	3	4

G 3. Sense that public officials pay attention to what people think.

Will decrease sense that public officials pay attention to what people think.	Unknown impact on sense that public officials pay attention to what people think.	Neutral impact on sense that public officials pay attention to what people think.	Will increase sense that public officials pay attention to what people think.
1	2	3	4

G 4. Proportion of population that attends peaceful demonstrations and frequency of signing petitions.

Will decrease proportion of population that attends peaceful demonstrations and frequency of signing petitions.	Unknown impact on proportion of population that attends peaceful demonstrations and frequency of signing petitions.	Neutral impact on proportion of population that attends peaceful demonstrations and frequency of signing petitions.	Will increase proportion of population that attends peaceful demonstrations and frequency of signing petitions.
1	2	3	4

G 5. Sense of confidence in local government.

Will decrease sense of confidence in local government.	Unknown impact on sense of confidence in local government.	Neutral impact on sense of confidence in local government.	Will increase sense of confidence in local government.
1	2	3	4

G 6. Proportion of civil society (population) participating in government process (e.g., urban planning and management, participatory budgeting, etc.) and frequency of participation.

Will decrease proportion of population participating in governmental process and frequency of participation.	Unknown impact on proportion of population participating in governmental process and frequency of participation.	Neutral impact on proportion of population participating in governmental process and frequency of participation.	Will increase proportion of population participating in governmental process and frequency of participation.
1	2	3	4

G 7. Sense of confidence in national government.

Will decrease sense of confidence in national government.	Unknown impact on sense of confidence in national government.	Neutral impact on sense of confidence in national government.	Will increase sense of confidence in national government.
1	2	3	4

G 8. Voter turnout.

Will decrease voter turnout.	Unknown impact on voter turnout.	Neutral impact on voter turnout.	Will increase voter turnout.
1	2	3	4

■ Standard of Living/ Economy (EC)

EC 1. Sense of stress about personal finances.

Will increase sense of stress about personal finances.	Unknown impact on sense of stress about personal finances.	Neutral impact on sense of stress about personal finances.	Will decrease people's sense of stress about personal finances.
1	2	3	4

EC 2. GINI Coefficient (measure of income or wealth distribution) for area.

Will increase the GINI coefficient.	Unknown impact on GINI coefficient.	Neutral impact on GINI coefficient.	Will decrease the GINI coefficient or maintain a low GINI coefficient.
1	2	3	4

EC 3. Experience of just getting by and living paycheck to paycheck.

Will increase frequency people experience just getting by and living paycheck to paycheck.	Unknown impact on frequency people experience just getting by and living paycheck to paycheck.	Neutral impact on frequency people experience just getting by and living paycheck to paycheck.	Will decrease frequency people experience just getting by and living paycheck to paycheck.
1	2	3	4

EC 4. Proportion of population living below the national poverty line, by sex and age.

Will increase proportion of population living below the national poverty line, by sex and age.	Unknown impact on proportion of population living below the national poverty line, by sex and age.	Neutral impact on proportion of population living below the national poverty line, by sex and age.	Will reduce proportion of population living below the national poverty line, by sex and age.
1	2	3	4

EC 5. Optimal average gross national income per capita for well-being in purchasing power parity.

Will decrease optimal average gross national income per capita for well-being in purchasing power parity.	Unknown impact on optimal average gross national income per capita for well-being in purchasing power parity.	Neutral impact on optimal average gross national income per capita for well-being in purchasing power parity.	Will achieve or maintain optimal average gross national income per capita for well-being in purchasing power parity.
1	2	3	4

EC 6. Experience of eating less because there wasn't enough food or money for food.

Will increase experience of eating less because there wasn't enough food or money for food.	Unknown impact on experience of eating less because there wasn't enough food or money for food.	Neutral impact on experience of eating less because there wasn't enough food or money for food.	Will decrease experience of eating less because there wasn't enough food or money for food.
1	2	3	4

EC 7. Access to safe, adequate, and nutritious food (e.g. Household Food Insecurity Access Scale —HFIAS) for diverse populations.

Will decrease access to safe, adequate, and nutritious food.	Unknown impact on access to safe, adequate, and nutritious food.	Neutral impact on access to safe, adequate, and nutritious food.	Will increase access to safe, adequate, and nutritious food.
1	2	3	4

EC 8. Sense of having enough money to buy things one wants.

Will decrease sense of having enough money to buy things one wants.	Unknown impact on sense of having enough money to buy things one wants.	Neutral impact on sense of having enough money to buy things one wants.	Will increase sense of having enough money to buy things one wants.
1	2	3	4

EC 9. Household expenditure (cost of housing and maintenance of the house, water, energy, furnishings, etc.).

Will increase household expenditure.	Unknown impact on household expenditure.	Neutral impact on household expenditure.	Will decrease household expenditure.
1	2	3	4

EC 10. Satisfaction with quality and affordability of housing.

Will decrease satisfaction with quality and affordability of housing.	Unknown impact on satisfaction with quality and affordability of housing.	Neutral impact on satisfaction with quality and affordability of housing.	Will increase satisfaction with quality and affordability of housing.
1	2	3	4

EC 11. Proportion of urban population living in slums, informal settlements, or inadequate housing.

Will increase proportion of urban population living in slums, informal settlements, or inadequate housing.	Unknown impact on proportion of urban population living in slums, informal settlements, or inadequate housing.	Neutral impact on proportion of urban population living in slums, informal settlements, or inadequate housing.	Will decrease proportion of urban population living in slums, informal settlements, or inadequate housing.
1	2	3	4

EC 12. Satisfaction with transportation system.

Will decrease satisfaction with transportation system.	Unknown impact on satisfaction with transportation system.	Neutral impact on satisfaction with transportation system.	Will increase satisfaction with transportation system.
1	2	3	4

EC 13. Proportion of population that has convenient access to public transport, by sex, age, and persons with disabilities.

Will decrease proportion of population that has convenient access to public transport, by sex, age, and persons with disabilities.	Unknown impact on proportion of population that has convenient access to public transport, by sex, age, and persons with disabilities.	Neutral impact on proportion of population that has convenient access to public transport, by sex, age, and persons with disabilities.	Will increase proportion of population that has convenient access to public transport, by sex, age, and persons with disabilities.
1	2	3	4

EC 14. Satisfaction with access to information and communication technologies (i.e. internet, wireless, mobile devices, etc.).

Will decrease satisfaction with access to information and communication technologies.	Unknown impact on satisfaction with access to information and communication technologies.	Neutral impact on satisfaction with access to information and communication technologies.	Will increase satisfaction with access to information and communication technologies.
1	2	3	4

EC 15. Proportion of population covered by a mobile network and with a cellular phone.

Will decrease proportion of population covered by a mobile network and with a cellular phone.	Unknown impact on proportion of population covered by a mobile network and with a cellular phone.	Neutral impact on proportion of population covered by a mobile network and with a cellular phone.	Will increase proportion of population covered by a mobile network and with a cellular phone.
1	2	3	4

■ Work (W)

W 1. Satisfaction with work.

Will decrease satisfaction with work.	Unknown impact on satisfaction with work.	Neutral impact on satisfaction with work.	Will increase satisfaction with work.
1	2	3	4

W 2. Unemployment rate.

Will increase unemployment rate.	Unknown impact on unemployment rate.	Neutral impact on unemployment rate.	Will decrease unemployment rate.
1	2	3	4

W 3. Labor market insecurity (the expected earnings loss, measured as the percentage of previous earnings, associated with unemployment).

Will increase labor market insecurity.	Unknown impact on labor market insecurity.	Neutral impact on labor market insecurity.	Will decrease labor market insecurity.
1	2	3	4

W 4. Satisfaction with work-life balance.

Will decrease satisfaction with work-life balance.	Unknown impact on satisfaction with work-life balance.	Neutral impact on satisfaction with work-life balance.	Will increase satisfaction with work-life balance.
1	2	3	4

W 5. Average commute times.

Will increase average commute times.	Unknown impact on average commute times.	Neutral impact on average commute times.	Will decrease average commute times.
1	2	3	4

W 6. Sense that current work life is interesting.

Will decrease sense that current work life is interesting.	Unknown impact on sense that current work life is interesting.	Neutral impact on sense that current work life is interesting.	Will increase sense that current work life is interesting.
1	2	3	4

W 7. Sense that conditions of one's job allow them to be about as productive as they could be.

Will decrease sense that conditions of one's job allow them to be about as productive as they could be.	Unknown impact on sense that conditions of one's job allow them to be about as productive as they could be.	Neutral impact on sense that conditions of one's job allow them to be about as productive as they could be.	Will increase sense that conditions of one's job allow them to be about as productive as they could be.
1	2	3	4

W 8. Sense of getting paid appropriately in one's job considering all one's efforts and achievements.

Will decrease sense of getting paid appropriately in one's job considering all one's efforts and achievements.	Unknown impact on sense of getting paid appropriately in one's job considering all one's efforts and achievements.	Neutral impact on sense of getting paid appropriately in one's job considering all one's efforts and achievements.	Will increase sense of getting paid appropriately in one's job considering all one's efforts and achievements.
1	2	3	4

W 9. Gender gap in wages, by sector of economic activity.

Will increase gender gap in wages.	Unknown impact on gender gap in wages.	Neutral impact on gender gap in wages.	Will decrease gender gap in wages.
1	2	3	4

W 10. Sense of autonomy at work (being allowed to decide to go about getting one's job done).

Will decrease sense of autonomy.	Unknown impact on sense of autonomy.	Neutral impact on sense of autonomy.	Will increase sense of autonomy.
1	2	3	4

Notes

Introduction

1. Lucy E. Edwards, "What Is the Anthropocene?" *EOS*, 2015. eos.org /opinions/what-is-the-anthropocene

2. Global Happiness Council, *Global Happiness and Well-Being Policy Report*, 2018. happinesscouncil.org/

3. John F. Helliwell, Richard Layard, and Jeffrey D. Sachs, eds., *World Happiness Report* (2012, 2013, 2015, 2016, 2017), Sustainable Development Solutions Network. worldhappiness.report/

4. Royal Government of Bhutan, *Defining a New Economic Paradigm: The Report of the High-Level Meeting on Wellbeing and Happiness*, Sustainable Development Solutions Network, 2012. sustainable development.un.org/index.php?page=view&type=400&nr=617 &menu=35

5. Gus O'Donnell, "Opening Address," conference on *Subjective Well-being Over the Life Course: Evidence and Policy Implications*, 2016. youtube.com/watch?v=wKmwweYJOnQ&list=PLyYjq-iDxl33T xq9hy8k4CAoY_bgpyOX

Chapter 1

1. Library of Congress, Thomas Jefferson to Washington County, Maryland, Republican Citizens, March 31, 1809. loc.gov/item/mtjbib 019889/

2. Simon Kuznets, European Commission, *Beyond GDP: Measuring Progress, True Wealth, and Well-being*, "Key quotes," (1934). ec.europa .eu/environment/beyond_gdp/key_quotes_en.html

3. The Constitution of the Kingdom of Bhutan, Article 9, clause 2, 2008. nationalcouncil.bt/assets/uploads/files/Constitution%20%20of%20 Bhutan%20English.pdf

4. Alejandro Adler, "Gross National Happiness in Bhutan: A Living Example of an Alternative Approach to Progress," *Social Impact Research Experience (SIRE)*, 2009. repository.upenn.edu/cgi/viewcontent.cgi

?referer=https://www.google.com/&httpsredir=1&article=1003&
context=sire

5. Joseph E. Stiglitz, Amartya Sen, and Jean-Paul Fitoussi, *Report by
the Commission on the Measurement of Economic Performance and
Social Progress*, 2009. ec.europa.eu/eurostat/documents/118025/118123
/Fitoussi+Commission+report

6. Organisation for Economic Co-operation and Development (OECD),
Better Life Index, 2018. oecdbetterlifeindex.org/

7. OECD. oecd.org/about/

8. United Kingdom Office for National Statistics, *Measuring national
well-being: domains and measures*, 2018. ons.gov.uk/peoplepopulation
andcommunity/wellbeing/datasets/measuringnationalwellbeing
domainsandmeasures

9. United Nations General Assembly, *Happiness: Towards a holistic
approach to development (Resolution 65/309)*, 2011. un.org/ga/search
/view_doc.asp?symbol=A/RES/65/309

10. Royal Government of Bhutan, *Defining a New Economic Paradigm:
Report of the High-Level Meeting on Wellbeing and Happiness*, 2012.
sustainabledevelopment.un.org/index.php?page=view&type=400
&nr=617&menu=35

11. Organisation for Economic Co-operation and Development, *OECD
Guidelines on Measuring Subjective Well-being*, 2013. dx.doi.org/10
.1787/9789264191655-en

12. Alistair Whitby, *The BRAINPOoL Project: Beyond GDP—From
Measurement to Politics and Policy*, 2014. semanticscholar.org/paper/T
he-BRAINPOoL-Project-%3A-Beyond-GDP-%E2%80%93-From-to
-and-Whitby/c2686831dd663623e713c496dc5ae236e52c63fd

13. Subjective well-being conference, 2016. youtube.com/playlist?list=PLy
Yjq-iDxl33Txq9hy8k4CAoY_bgpyOXO

14. World Government Summit, *Global Dialogue for Happiness and Well-
being*. worldgovernmentsummit.org/initiatives/forums

15. Happiness Council, *Global Happiness and Well-Being Policy Report*,
2018. happinesscouncil.org/

16. Alistair Whitby, *The BRAINPOoL Project*.

Chapter 2

1. Rhonda Phillips and Robert Pittman, eds., *An Introduction to Community Development*, Routledge, 2015.

2. For a more comprehensive exploration of community well-being, see
Rhonda Phillips and Cecilia Wong, eds., *Handbook of Community*

Well-Being Research, Springer, 2017, or Seung Jong Lee, Yunyi Kim, and Rhonda Phillips, eds., *Community Well-Being and Community Development, Conceptions and Applications,* Springer, 2015.

3. Richard A. Easterlin, "Does Economic Growth Improve the Human Lot? Some Empirical Evidence," in Paul A. David and Melvin W. Reder, eds., *Nations and Households in Economic Growth: Essays in Honor of Moses Abramowitz,* Academic Press, 2014, pp. 89–125. graphics8.nytimes.com/images/2008/04/16/business/Easterlin1974 .pdf; R. Easterlin, "Will Raising the Incomes of All Increase the Happiness of All?" *Journal of Economic Behavior and Organization,* 27, 1995, 35–48.; R. Easterlin, "Income and Happiness: Towards a Unified Theory," *The Economic Journal,* 111, 2001, 465–484.; Richard Layard, *Happiness: Lessons from a New Science,* Penguin Books, 2006.

4. Gus O'Donnell, et al., *Wellbeing and Policy,* Legatum Institute, 2014. li.com/wp.../commission-on-wellbeing-and-policy-report-march-2014 -pdf.pdf

5. Richard A. Easterlin, "Income and Happiness"; Richard A. Easterlin, "Will Raising the Incomes of All Increase the Happiness of All?"

6. BBC Magazine Monitor, *Who, What, Why: What is the Gini coefficient?* March 12, 2015. bbc.com/news/blogs-magazine-monitor -31847943

7. Richard Wilkinson and Kate Pickett, *The Spirit Level: Why Greater Equality Makes Societies Stronger,* Bloomsbury Press, 2001.

8. Richard Layard, "Mental Illness Destroys Happiness And Is Costless To Treat," in Jeffrey Sachs, et. al., *Global Happiness Policy Report,* (Chapter 3), Sustainable Development Solutions Network. s3.amazon aws.com/ghc-2018/GHC_Ch3.pdf

9. R. T. Howell, P. Pchelin, and R. Iyer, "The Preference for Experiences Over Possessions: Measurement and Construct Validation of the Experiential Buying Tendency Scale," *The Journal of Positive Psychology,* 7.1 (2012): p. 57–71.

10. Lara B. Aknin, et al., "Making a Difference Matters: Impact Unlocks the Emotional Benefits of Prosocial Spending," *Journal of Economic Behavior & Organization,* 88 (2013): p. 90–95.

11. David Suzuki, *One of the worst words in the dictionary,* 2018. davidsuzuki.org/story/one-of-the-worst-words-in-the-dictionary/

12. Bureau of Economic Analysis, Chapter 5: "Personal Consumption Expenditure," *NIPA Handbook: Concepts and Methods of the U.S. National Income and Product Accounts,* 2017. bea.gov/sites/default/files /methodologies/nipa-handbook-all-chapters.pdf#page=90

13. Victor Lebow, "Price competition in 1955." *Journal of Retailing*, 1955. gcafh.org/edlab/Lebow.pdf

14. Andrew K. Jorgenson, "Consumption and Environmental Degradation: A Cross-National Analysis of the Ecological Footprint," *Social Problems* 50, 3 (2003): 374–394.

Chapter 3

1. United Nations. *UN Climate Change Annual Report 2017*. unfccc.int /resource/annualreport/

2. Intergovernmental Panel on Climate Change (IPCC) *Summary for Policy Makers*. 2018. report.ipcc.ch/sr15/pdf/sr15_spm_final.pdf

3. For more information regarding community indicators, see Rhonda Phillips, *Community Indicators*, PAS Report No. 517, American Planning Association; Rhonda Phillips, *Community Indicator Measuring Systems*, Ashgate Publishing; or any of the *Community Quality-of-Life Indicators: Best Cases* series by Springer.

4. World Government Summit, *Discovering Indonesia's Happiness Pyramid – H. E. Bambang Brodjonegoro*. February 10, 2018. youtube .com/watch?v=trCG6UViYq4 (minutes 12:40 – 13:00)

Chapter 4

1. Abraham H. Maslow, "A Theory of Human Motivation," *Psychological Review*, 50(4) (1943): 370–396.

2. Beth Azar, "Positive Psychology Advances, with Growing Pains," *American Psychological Association*, 24, 4 (2011): 32. apa.org/monitor /2011/04/positive-psychology.aspx

3. Sonja Lyubomirsky, *The How of Happiness: A Scientific Approach to Getting the Life You Want*. Penguin, 2008; Jan-Emmanuel De Neve, et al., "Genes, economics, and happiness," *Journal of Neuroscience, Psychology, and Economics*, 5, 4 (2012): 193–211.

4. Julia K. Boehm and Sonja Lyubomirsky, "Does happiness promote career success?" *Journal of Career Assessment*, 16, 1 (2018): 101–106.

5. Robert E. Quinn, and Anjan V. Thakor, "Creating a Purpose-Driven Organization," *Harvard Business Review*, 2018, 79–85. hbr.org/2018/07/ creating-a-purpose-driven-organization

Chapter 7

1. The Constitution of the Kingdom of Bhutan (2008). Article IX, Clause II. nationalcouncil.bt/assets/uploads/docs/acts/2017/Consti tution_of_Bhutan_2008.pdf

2. Republic of Ecuador, "Chapter Seven: Rights of Nature," *Constitution of the Republic of Ecuador*, 2008. pdba.georgetown.edu/Constitutions /Ecuador/english08.html

3. Office for National Statistics, "Reinventing the 'Well-Being Wheel,'" 2017. blog.ons.gov.uk/2017/03/28/national-statistical-blog-reinventing -the-well-being-wheel/

4. Laura Musikanski and Carl Polley, "Life, Liberty, and the Pursuit of Happiness: Measuring What Matters," *Journal of Social Change*, 8, 1 (2016): 48–72.

5. World Government Summit, *Discovering Indonesia's Happiness Pyramid*.

6. Gus O'Donnell et al., *Well-being and Policy*, Legatum Institute, 2014. li.com/docs/default-source/commission-on-well-being-and-policy/c ommission-on-well-being-and-policy-report---march-2014-pdf.pdf; New Economics Foundation, Karen Jeffrey and Juliet Michaelson, *Five Headline Indicators of National Success*, 2015. b.3cdn.net/nefoun dation/1ff58cfc7d3f4b3fad_04m6ynyiz.pdf

7. Laura Musikanski, "Happiness in public policy," *Journal of Social Change*, 6, (2014): 55–85. scholarworks.waldenu.edu/jsc/vol6/iss1/5/

8. Laura Musikanski, "Why a Muslim Nation May Save the World or the Rising Middle Power of Happiness," *The Solutions Journal*, 9, 3 (July 2018). thesolutionsjournal.com/article/muslim-nation-may-save -world-rising-middle-power-happiness/

9. IANS, "Inspired by Bhutan, Madhya Pradesh to create 'department of happiness' to keep its citizens stress-free." *Firstpost*. April 24, 2016. firstpost.com/india/inspired-by-bhutan-madhya-pradesh-to-create -department-of-happiness-to-keep-its-citizens-stress-free-2707626 .html

Chapter 8

1. The Well-being Project City of Santa Monica, "Panel of experts," p. 3 wellbeing.smgov.net/about/partners-and-panel

2. *Arabian Business*, "UAE creates first World Happiness Council," March 20 2017. arabianbusiness.com/uae-creates-first-world-happi ness-council-667662.html

3. Victoria Foundation, *The Happiness Index Partnership*, 2017. victoria foundation.bc.ca/past-initiatives/happiness-index-partnership/

4. Wam, "Mohammad bin Rashid Smart Majlis receives 35,000 ideas," *Emirates 24/7*, January 2017. emirates247.com/news/emirates/moham med-bin-rashid-smart-majlis-receives-35-000-ideas-2017-01-22-1 .646848

5. World Government Summit (February 10, 2018). *Global Dialogue for Happiness: Towards a Happier Life*. Retrieved from worldgovernment summit.org/initiatives/forums/global-dialogue-for-happiness-2018

6. Laura Musikanski et al., "Happiness in Communities: How Neighborhoods, Cities, and States Use Subjective Well-Being Metrics," *Journal of Social Change* 9, 2017, (1): 32–54.

7. KCTS Connects, Season 5, Episode 509 (February 25 2011). pbs.org /video/kcts-9-connects-february-25-2011/

Chapter 9

1. Ed Diener et al., "New Measures of Well-Being," *Social Indicators Research*, 39, (2009): 247–266. mysmu.edu/faculty/williamtov/pubs /2009_DienerEtAl.pdf

2. Daniel Kahneman, et al., "When More Pain Is Preferred to Less: Adding a Better End," *Psychological Science*. 4 (1993): 401–405.

3. Felicia A. Huppert and Timothy T. C. So, "Flourishing Across Europe: Application of a New Conceptual Framework for Defining Well-Being," *Social Indicators Research*, 110, 3 (2011): 837–861.

4. KCTS 9 Connects, Season 5 Episode 508, 2011. video.kcts9.org/video /kcts-9-connects-february-25-2011/

5. Daniel Fisher, "A Look at New York City's Participatory Budgeting Map," *Government Technology: Digital Communities*, 2018. govtech .com/dc/A-Look-at-New-York-Citys-Participatory-Budgeting-Map .html

6. Department of Communities and Local Government, "Communities in the driving seat: a study of Participatory Budgeting in England Final Report," 2011. assets.publishing.service.gov.uk/government /uploads/system/uploads/attachment_data/file/6152/19932231.pdf

7. Ed Diener, Richard Lucas, Ulrich Schimmack, and John Helliwell, *Well-Being for Public Policy*, Oxford University Press, 2011.

8. Ed Diener, et al., "New Measures of Well-Being."

9. For a random sampling, the equation to calculate sample size is $\{z^2 \times p[1-p]/e^2\}/\{1+[z^2 \times p(1-p)/e^2 \times N]\}$ where N is the size of the population, e is the margin of error stated in decimal form, and z is the z-score which is the number of standard deviations from the mean. For a confidence level of 95%, you use a z score of 1.96. Thus, for a confidence level of 95% and margin of error of 2, a sample size of 1,937 is needed for a population of 10,000, or 2,345 for a population of 100,000 and of 2,396 for a population of 1 million.

10. L. Musikanski, et al., (2017). "Happiness Index Methodology," *Journal for Social Change* 9, 2017.

Chapter 10

1. Karma Ura, (2015). *The Experience of Gross National Happiness as Development Framework*, Asian National Bank. adb.org/sites/default /files/publication/177790/gnh-development-framework.pdf

2. Karma Ura and Dorji Penjore, *GNH Policy and Project Selection Tools*, The Centre for Bhutan Studies, 2008. grossnationalhappiness.com /docs/GNH/PPT/Pol&Pro_Scr_Tools.ppt

3. Laura Musikanski, "Happiness in Public Policy," *Journal for Social Change* 6, 1 (2014): 55–85.

4. Centre for Bhutan Studies and GNH. *GNH Tools*, 2008. grossnationalhappiness.com/gnh-policy-and-project-screening-tools/

5. *The National*, "UAE launches Happiness Policy Manual," October 28, 2017. thenational.ae/uae/uae-launches-happiness-policy-manual -1.670946

Appendix B

1. Paul Grossman, et al., "Mindfulness-based Stress Reduction and Health Benefits. A Meta-analysis," *Journal of Psychosomatic Research*, 57 1 (2004): 35–42.

2. Michael Dambrun and Matthieu Ricard, "Self-centeredness and Selflessness: A Theory of Self-based Psychological Functioning and Its Consequences for Happiness," *Review of General Psychology*, 5, 2 (2011): 138–157; Barbara L. Fredrickson, "The role of positive emotions in positive psychology: The broaden-and-build theory of positive emotions," *The American Psychologist*, 56, 3 (2001): 218–226.

3. Barbara L. Fredrickson, et al., "Open Hearts Build Lives: Positive Emotions, Induced Through Loving-kindness Meditation, Build Consequential Personal Resources," *Journal of Personality and Social Psychology*, 95, 5 (November 2008): 1045–1062.

4. Philip C. Watkins, et al., "Gratitude and Happiness: Development of a Measure of Gratitude, and Relationships with Subjective Well-Being," *Social Behavior and Personality: An International Journal*, 31, 5 (2003): 431–451.

5. Robert A. Emmons, and Michael E. McCollough. "Counting Blessings Versus Burdens: An Experimental Investigation of Gratitude and Subjective Well-Being in Daily Life," *Journal of Personality and Social*

Psychology, 84, 2 (2003): 377–389. greatergood.berkeley.edu/images/application_uploads/Emmons-CountingBlessings.pdf

6. Soyoung Q. Park et al., "A Neural Link Between Generosity and Happiness," *Nature Communications* 8, 2017.

Appendix C

1. The Community Toolbox. ctb.ku.edu/en
2. Charles Dobson, *The Troublemaker's Teaparty: A Manual for Effective Citizen Action*, New Society Publishers, 2003.
3. Nick Licata, *Becoming a Citizen Activist: Stories, Strategies & Advice for Changing Our World*, Sasquatch Books, 2016.

Index

Page numbers in *italics* indicate figures.

About the Authors

LAURA MUSIKANSKI is executive director of the Happiness
Alliance, co-founder of Planet Happiness, and chair of IEEE
P7010—The Well-being Metrics Standard for Autonomous and
Intelligent Systems. She is on the editorial board of the International Journal of Community Well-being and author of two
books—*Sustainability Decoded* and *How to Account for Sustain-*
ability. Laura was an invited participant at the 2012 UN High Level Meeting
on Well-being and Happiness: Defining a New Economic Paradigm where
the Ad-Hoc Global Happiness and Well-being Movement Group, which
she leads and coordinates, first convened. She lives in Seattle WA.

RHONDA PHILLIPS is a community well-being, development,
and planning specialist and Dean of Purdue Honors College.
She has conduced hand-on research with policy makers, community organizers and academia for over 30 years. She is author
or editor of 25 books, including the Handbook of Community
Well-being Research. She is co-founder of the Springer jour-
nal, International Journal of Community Well-Being and past president of
the International Society of Quality-of-Life Studies. Her many awards and
honors include three Fulbright awards. Rhonda is a Happiness Alliance
Board Member and lives in Lafayette, IN.

JEAN CROWDER served as a member of parliament (MP) in the
Canadian government between 2004–2015, and has extensive
experience as a policymaker. She worked for Human Resources
Development Canada, the British Columbia Ministry of Skills
Training and Labour, and was a human resources consultant
and manager at Malaspina University College. Crowder is a
Happiness Alliance board member and lives in Duncan, BC.

ABOUT NEW SOCIETY PUBLISHERS

New Society Publishers is an activist, solutions-oriented publisher focused on publishing books for a world of change. Our books offer tips, tools, and insights from leading experts in sustainable building, homesteading, climate change, environment, conscientious commerce, renewable energy, and more—positive solutions for troubled times.

We're proud to hold to the highest environmental and social standards of any publisher in North America. This is why some of our books might cost a little more. We think it's worth it!

DON'T EAT THIS BOOK *(but you could)*

- We print all our books in North America, never overseas

- All our books are printed on **100% post-consumer recycled paper**, processed chlorine-free, with low-VOC vegetable-based inks (since 2002)

- Our corporate structure is an innovative employee shareholder agreement, so we're one-third employee-owned (since 2015)

- We're carbon-neutral (since 2006)

- We're certified as a B Corporation (since 2016)

At New Society Publishers, we care deeply about *what* we publish—but also about *how* we do business.

Download our catalog at https://newsociety.com/Our-Catalog or for a printed copy please email info@newsocietypub.com or call 1-800-567-6772 ext 111.

New Society Publishers
ENVIRONMENTAL BENEFITS STATEMENT

For every 5,000 books printed, New Society saves the following resources:[1]

23	Trees
2,120	Pounds of Solid Waste
2,333	Gallons of Water
3,043	Kilowatt Hours of Electricity
3,854	Pounds of Greenhouse Gases
17	Pounds of HAPs, VOCs, and AOX Combined
6	Cubic Yards of Landfill Space

[1] Environmental benefits are calculated based on research done by the Environmental Defense Fund and other members of the Paper Task Force who study the environmental impacts of the paper industry.

Certified
Corporation

FSC
www.fsc.org

MIX
Paper from responsible sources
FSC® C016245

new society
P U B L I S H E R S
www.newsociety.com